THE REAL GUIDE TO SURVEILLANCE

(SECOND EDITION)

By Michael Chandler

UNDERSTANDING THE INTRICACIES OF FOOT AND MOBILE SURVEILLANCE IS A VITAL ATTRIBUTE FOR ANY CLOSE PROTECTION OFFICER. KNOWING HOW COVERT OPERATIVES/ TEAMS FUNCTION, METHODS OF COMMUNICATION, THE FOOT DRILLS THAT THEY ADOPT, IS KEY AND CAN ONLY REALLY BE UNDERSTOOD BY SOMEONE WHO HAS BEEN TRAINED TO A HIGH STANDARD. WITHOUT IT, YOUR PRINCIPAL WILL BE VULNERABLE TO SURVEILLANCE WHETHER THAT BE HOSTILE RECONNAISSANCE OR COVERT INTELLIGENCE ACQUISITION RELATING TO THEIR DAILY MOVEMENTS (PATTERN OF LIFE) IN AN EFFORT TO ESTABLISH WEAK POINTS WITHIN THE SECURITY ARRANGEMENTS. IDENTIFYING SUCH ACTIVITIES WILL MITIGATE THIS RISK CONSIDERABLY THUS PROVIDING A FAR MORE SECURE ENVIRONMENT FOR THEM.

CONTENTS

ABOUT THE AUTHOR

Michael Chandler is a retired bodyguard who now works primarily as a security consultant and training instructor. Having authored numerous courses and publications relating to security and intelligence acquisition, he travels the world teaching existing and aspiring security operatives as well as consulting high-net-worth individuals/ families and corporate clients on personal, residential and corporate security.

Michael Chandler working as a CPO (*Daily Mail Online, 2012*)

Born and raised in London, Michael served in the Royal Military Police (TA), the regiment that fulfils close protection roles within the British Army. He then went on to work for investigation firms along with security companies simultaneously as a freelancer. As a result, he spent many years working in large security teams on high profile events such as film premieres and award ceremonies. During this time he was also conducting covert counter-surveillance operations in and around the London area as a trainee, later progressing to operations across the UK. This led to a promotion giving him the title 'Head of International Surveillance Operations' for a large private contractor.

Naturally progressing in his career, Michael went on to work with various recording artists and actors in a close protection capacity later evolving to consult and advise other security companies on anti & counter-surveillance matters along with providing any investigative services they required in order to identify the origins of threats.

Because of his history of working on large scale investigations, Michael's career evolved into one that saw him being engaged by high net worth families and individuals who had received some form of threat. This ultimately led to the release of the intelligence acquisition based Vanquish Close Protection Course which is made up of investigative based courses (made available to the public years before), combined with the bodyguard element, all of which were written by Chandler.

Now, Michael is the Chief Operating Officer of The Vanquish® Group which owns and manages Vanquish® Security Services, Vanquish® Investigation Services and Vanquish® Training Academy. He is also the author of the International seller 'The Real Guide to Surveillance' which sells in most English speaking countries including; UK, Australia, New Zealand, Canada and The US.

Vanquish® still advises other security companies on counter surveillance and investigative matters. Their other corporate clients include law firms solicitors, private individuals, employment agencies, retailers, the BBC and Universal Records. Michael has written all of our courses himself for which people come from all over the world to attend.

INTRODUCTION

This book was originally written from a two day basic surveillance training course that I wrote as a result of an apparent lack of properly trained surveillance operative in the private sector. The original (first edition) book was put together within a very short timeframe. I set a goal to have it completed before Christmas 2011 but due to numerous work related commitments, only managed to start in late November of the same year. As a result, the book was rushed and, in all honesty, not very well composed. This second edition is not only an updated version but also one that is inclusive of far more detail. It includes more content from the five day advance surveillance course which I finished writing in 2013. I have spent some time reconsidering the chronology of the content in an effort to make it more succinct with the overall topic. Another aspect in which I have attempted to improve is the timelessness of the publication. That is, I have endeavoured to resist the urge of referring to specific, current technology because it will affect how this book is perceived in the future. Writing about aspects of technology that are current at the time of writing a book often proves worthless within a matter of years, sometimes even months at the rate in which technology is moving in this day and age. There are elements, as you will find throughout this book, that simply could not be avoided. I refer specifically to SLR cameras and how vehicle tracking devices currently function. The remainder relates to legislation (which will also change as time progresses) alongside covert foot surveillance techniques, mobile surveillance techniques, peripheral awareness, conscious and subconscious memory and many other aspects which, in theory, should remain the same.

If you are someone who has previously been involved with covert surveillance then you may discover that you have already taken on some of the methods discussed in this book but was not sure of their formal titles. Similarly, if you were to be deployed on a surveillance task for the first time, you may find yourself instinctively adopting them. This book will serve as a reminder as to the names, methods, benefits and when to utilise such drills. It will also be beneficial to anyone who is unsure of the relevant legislation in the UK and how it impacts us as private contractors in comparison with public bodies such as local authorities, the police and intelligence services. You will also consider the various types of covert equipment that is available to surveillance operatives, their functions, benefits and downsides. This will be inclusive of the various forms of communications including formal two way radio etiquette. Given that photography is a huge part of covert observations, this will also be discussed in quite some detail. More specifically, we will look into SLR cameras, different types of lenses and the various settings that are available to ensure that the imagery that the operative takes is of the highest standard and usable for evidential purposes. In relation to evidence, we will also consider the art of report writing highlighting common errors that others make in the arena and how to avoid them. I will draw from relevant material pertaining to how public services write their reports combined with my experience in the Royal Military Police (TA) and as 'Head of International Surveillance

Operations' for a private organisation. It's all here and if properly digested, you will be able to write a competent surveillance report that is able to withstand the robust cross examination of a defence barrister, should your evidence ever make it to Crown Court. In addition to all of the above, you will gain further insight as to how operational briefings are constructed in an effort to later enable you to plan, prepare, brief and execute your own surveillance ops.

My previous book, Technical Surveillance Countermeasures and the course that accompanied it resulted in the first bug sweeping course in the private sector, ever to be held in Australia and then Ghana. Owing to this, I spent a lot of time travelling in 2019 - the year the book was released. As a result of my travels (and my inability to switch off from work) this book was composed in London, Birmingham, Manchester, Lisbon, Accra, Cape Verde, New Delhi, Singapore, Taipei, Sydney, San Francisco, thirty eight thousand feet above the Atlantic and Pacific oceans and the South China Sea.

This is a book in which I do not intend on making a third edition of and so hope to make this edition a more relevant, succinct, referrable and finalised version. I hope you enjoy reading it as much as I have enjoyed writing it.

Throughout the book two fictitious scenarios will be given where necessary. One will pertain to a matrimonial case which is by far one of the most common grounds for surveillance in the private sector. The other will relate to an insurance claim which, again, is a very common reason for companies to instruct surveillance operations. This should provide a good contrast between the two main client types in the private sector; private clients (individuals) and corporate clients (businesses/ companies). The private matrimonial operation will be referred to as “OP LUMA’ and the corporate insurance task as “OP INDIA CHARLIE”.

Some of the techniques are demonstrated using two dimensional diagrams whilst others are done utilising photographs in an effort to illustrate them in a realistic setting. To make it easy for the positions to be indicated, they will be done using black figures to denote the operative(s) positions and red to highlight that of the subject’s.

Figure 3

In the two dimensional diagrams, the subject will be marked with a red “S” inside a red circle accompanied by an arrow to show the direction of travel.

Figure 4

The subject’s positions will be denoted with the letters “A”, “B” or “C” inside black circles.

Figure 5

THE HISTORY OF VANQUISH® TRAINING ACADEMY

Vanquish Security & Investigation Consultants Ltd was set up in 2011 to provide security services to celebrities and high net worth individuals. Because the security industry is very competitive, they chose to include investigation services so that if any of their clients received a threat, they could investigate that threat to identify where it was coming from as opposed to just simply providing more security personnel. Later in 2011, Vanquish decided to open their investigative services to the general public purchasing ThePrivateInvestigators.co.uk and later winning ThePrivateInvestigators.com from the United States of America after a lengthy bidding war.

They already had a number of security operatives but now they needed surveillance operatives. According to the SIA, surveillance training must be included as part of a close protection course. The reality is that most have only attended a twelve day course where surveillance will only make up approximately half an hour of the syllabus. The result? Not a great deal of skill or knowledge when it came to surveillance. Vanquish® noticed that the work quality and report writing abilities of their operatives was somewhere between average and very very poor. For this precise reason, Michael Chandler decided to write a surveillance training course outlining basic techniques, standard operating procedures, report writing and legislation. All Vanquish® operatives were invited to the free 2 day course in the hope that there would be some form of unity between them and their surveillance reports. It worked. The work quality and the quality of the reports (which are received by the clients), improved considerably. Almost immediately after the short number of courses, the head office started receiving requests to hold more courses for the friends and colleagues of the existing Vanquish® operatives who stated that their friends were willing to pay. This was when Vanquish® Training Academy was born. In 2013, the investigation business made a decision that they would only ever recruit those who had done one of their own surveillance courses, not as a money making exercise, but to ensure that tasks are being conducted properly and professionally. As of August 2016, the security company adopted exactly the same recruitment policy.

Since then, Vanquish® Security and Vanquish® Investigation Services have become separate companies but are still managed by The Vanquish® Group.

(Police Resettlement Magazine, 2016)

TERMINOLOGY

In any industry that a person works in, they will inevitably be introduced to what may be unfamiliar words or phrases that are colloquially used within that sector. The security industry is no different. With this industry being made up predominantly of ex-military and ex-police personnel, much of the terminology derives from those professions. It is important, therefore to highlight some that are utilised, more specifically, in the investigation or surveillance sector.

WA - Work Address. Often pertaining to the 'work address' of a subject.

HA - Home Address.

Fox-Trot - This basically means to go on foot. Not my favourite expression as 'Gone on Fox-Trot' has more syllables than simply 'on foot'.

RV - RV is short for the French word rendezvous which means to 'meet up'.

Recce - This is short for another French word, reconnaissance. A recce, also known as recon by our American friends, is an exercise which is carried out in order to ascertain as much information about the area, location or building of where a surveillance operation will take place.

Subject - The subject is the person on which we are mounting observations, also known as SOE.

SOE - SOE is an abbreviation for Subject of Enquiry. This is the person on whom we are mounting an investigation or surveillance operation on.

Int/ Intel - Short for intelligence, Intel is vital pieces of information that is gathered during or before an operation.

Comms - Short for communications, comms are vital to the operational team. Comms can be in several forms including mobile phone and two way radio.

End Ex - End Ex is short for end of exercise and in English, it basically means stop. Finish what you are doing and leave the area.

Eyes On - Eyes on means to have a current visual of the subject.

Third Party Aware - This means that someone is aware of surveillance operatives and or they are aware that someone may be following them.

Loc Stat - Short for 'Location Status', Loc Stat is usually asked as a question. This is the shorter way of asking "where are you"?

The Ground - The ground is the area in which your operation is taking place.

Compromised - This is when the surveillance has been seen by the subject or when another third party has notified the subject of your presence.

Sit Rep - Sit Rep is short for 'Situation Report' which is military way for asking for an update.

LUP - Lay Up Point. This is discussed later on in some detail.

IR - Infra Red

ERV - Emergency Rendezvous Point

PPE - Personal Protective Equipment

Trigger - The trigger is a position within a surveillance team. We go over this in more detail later on.

Med Kit - Medical Kit

Alpha(s) - People

Bravo(s) - Vehicles

Charlie(s) - Buildings

VRN - Vehicle Registration Number

GPS - Global Positioning System

HQ - Head Quarters. The head office of the investigation company you are working for or the main operations room.

Bug Out - This means leave the area or building.

SOPs - Standard Operating Procedures. These are implemented usually by the company who is in charge of the task. Later in the book we will go through some of our own SOPs as well as some basic ones that you should consider adopting.

Unit - or 'units' typically refer to vehicles whether that be motorcycles, cars or vans to assist the facilitation of a covert surveillance operation.

ROLES & RESPONSIBILITIES

We are now going to outline the roles and responsibilities of a covert surveillance operative in the private sector. Roles and responsibilities are subjective from company to company. This chapter will not consider the intricacies of how all companies may operate. Instead it will discuss some of those adopted by Vanquish in the hope that it will shed some light onto how third party organisations may work and provide a small amount of commercial insight.

Before going through them one by one, it is worth pointing out that some of the these bullet points are very brief. Some of them are self explanatory and others will explored in greater detail later on.

Reading and understanding operational briefings

Prior to an operative being deployed, they will receive an operational briefing. The operational briefing will outline certain details about the task. Once that briefing has been received, it is the operative's responsibility to understand the it in full. If there is something that they do not understand then they need to communicate with the company who delegates it to them.

Planning & preparing for your deployment

Operatives are expected to have, at the very least, some basic kit of their own. The operative then needs to ensure that all of that kit is properly charged and prepared prior to their deployment. It may sound silly but, the journey should also be planned and/ or researched beforehand to ensure that there are no missed opportunities in respect of the objectives.

Your own health & safety

You will see later on that you are legally responsible for your own health and safety and why.

Conducting the operation in a competent manner

Operatives are responsible for carrying out a task in a competent and legal manner. This is another one that example that does not require an extensive explanation.

Writing a comprehensive report and sending it to HQ

As a trained individual you will go through relatively extensive report writing skills and therefore as a result it is your responsibility and part of your role to write a comprehensive report and sending it back to HQ. We will cover this in relatively extensive detail later on.

Being knowledgeable in the subject matter

By attending a training course, you will become knowledgeable and you will gain expertise. However, it is your responsibility to do is develop what we refer to as CPD or 'continuous professional development'. We will go over this later on in more detail but for now, it refers to your continuous research into the technology, legislation and other factors that impact you or your work in any given field. So as a surveillance operative, you should endeavour to continuously update your knowledge on new technology that is available to you for the purpose of using technical surveillance and the laws that make it lawful or unlawful for you to do so.

SPECIALIST EQUIPMENT

The equipment that is available to surveillance operatives will change and evolve over time. In order to maintain a level of continuous professional development, operatives are recommended to research new technology as and when it becomes available. Over the following pages we will discuss one of the more prominent contraptions along with other items that fall within the category of ‘technical surveillance’.

Body-worn Cameras

Covert body-worn cameras have been used since the 1970s. They are likely to evolve as time goes on in terms of size, recording ability and memory capability but it is inconceivable that we will stop using them in the foreseeable future. Since the first edition of this book, they have already evolved from a product consisting of a camera with a relatively bulky recording unit to a much smaller combined battery, recording and camera unit.

Such devices allow an operative to covertly record audio and video footage which can later be used as evidence. It is worth noting that images can be taken from the video footage for reporting purposes.

The most common type of covert body-worn cameras come in

the form of buttons. These are ones that are concealed as buttons on a shirt. Other come in the form of spectacles, hats and wrist watches.

Figure 7 - Body-worn button camera *(Lawmate, 2020a)*

Figure 8 - Covert spectacles camera (*Lawmate, 2020b*)

Technical Surveillance

Technical surveillance can be defined as 'any covert monitoring device that uses technology to acquire footage or data of someone's movements.' In other words, a bug is something that secretly captures audio, video or still footage. As a surveillance operative, these devices are available to you but must be used within the boundaries of the law.

The following paragraphs are taken from the book *Technical Surveillance Countermeasures*

TECHNICAL SURVEILLANCE

We will now examine what a bug actually is. Because of the films, books and other forms of fiction which have gone on to promote spying and covert monitoring, there are consequently some misconceptions as to what a bug actually is. In essence, a bug is anything that enables a third party to covertly monitor or record a person or group of people. I often hear people say that a bugging device is "only one that can listen" or "a bugging device is one that you can remotely monitor" and so on. Technically speaking, it is something that allows you to covertly monitor someone. Monitoring doesn't have to necessarily be *live* monitoring.

There are primarily five main types of what are commonly referred to as "bugs":

- Recording devices
- Listening devices
- Covert or hidden cameras
- Vehicle tracking devices
- Wiretaps

Recording Devices

Recording devices are those that are deployed into a desired location but have to be extracted in order to review the footage. The simple fact that it records is the easiest way to remember it and its functions. It has to be removed in order for the end user to benefit from that footage. A recording device can come in many sizes and different shapes as long as there's enough room for a microphone, a power source and a SD card which is where the recorded footage will be stored.

In figure 9, you will see a slightly misleading image of the technology that is available to us. It is a very small circuit board comprising of a number of even smaller components, one of which is a microphone. The reason that I said “misleading”, was because the person who is holding the device is concealing the largest and arguably the most important part of the product. You will see the two wires leading from the circuit board disappear between his or her fingers. I know it is a black and white photograph but, the slightly lighter coloured lead is actually red and the dark coloured one is black, both of which lead to a nine volt battery. So this photograph is quite interesting because it looks like it might be a marketing image to market the kind of technology that the company is trying to promote. However, the reality is the power source and the battery increases the size of that device considerably. I don't know why we as a human race are able to send satellites around the globe, rockets and exploration mechanisms to different planets and yet we cannot manage to significantly reduce the size of batteries.

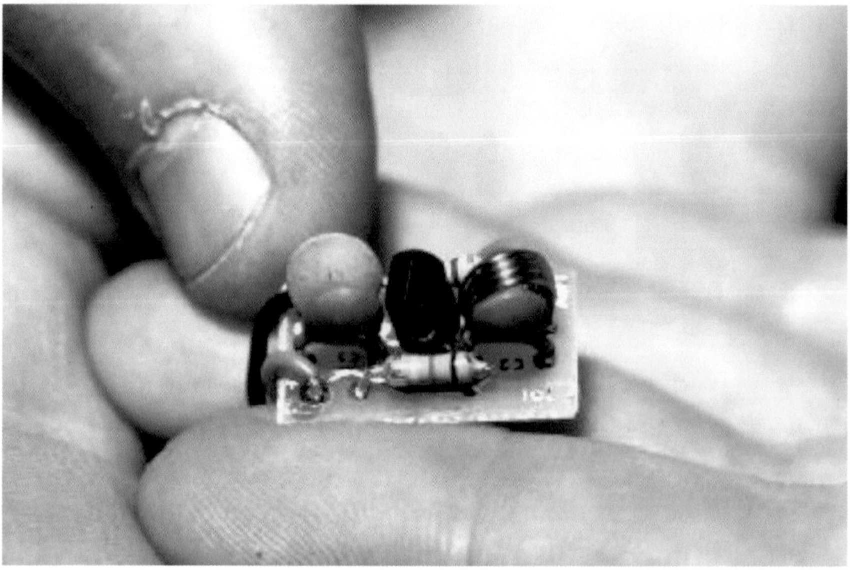

Figure 9

Listening Devices

A listening device is a unit which is used to monitor an area, room or individual from a remote location. This type of device will emit a radio frequency or cellular signal which is something that we are going to explore in a lot more detail later on but for now, just be mindful that of this fact. Whilst not trying to come across as patronizing or condescending, the easiest way to remember its function is that, a listening device is one that enables you to proactively listen.

The type and strength of the signal from the device will vary if it works using a radio frequency and the distance between the device itself and the receiver will also vary depending on the strength of the signal. As you can see in figure 10 a high frequency device will require the end user to be relatively nearby. Lower frequency signals travel further than higher frequency signals which is a little bit of a paradox. I have included a picture of a van in this image to depict what you have probably seen in numerous film productions whereby FBI or CIA agents are sat inside a van outside of a property relatively close by listening to what's going on. A higher frequency device will require a receiving unit relatively close by which can be to listen, record or both. It can be concealed in some way but should be accessible to the person monitoring.

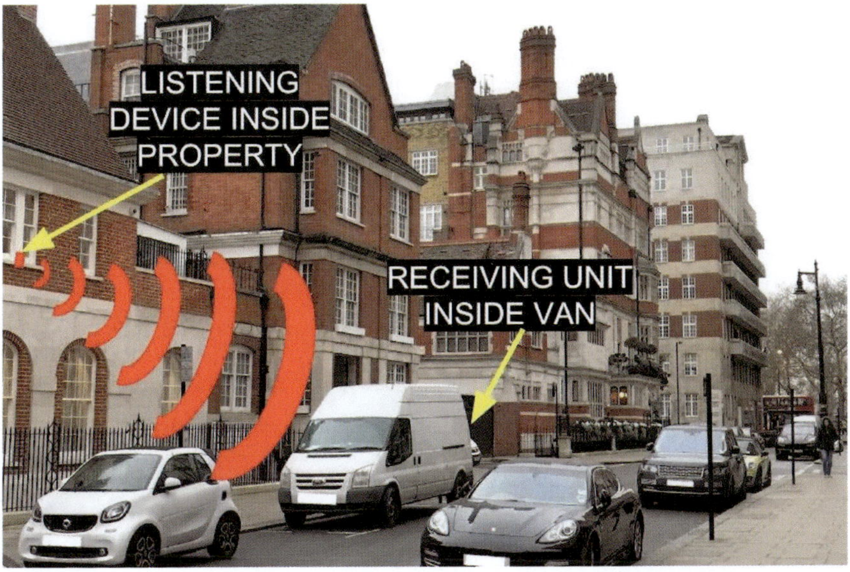

Figure 10

If you can imagine a scenario whereby an individual manages to plant a listening device inside a room where they intend to monitor. They will need to record the conversation or the footage that is occurring within the room in which they are monitoring on a different recording unit to that device. They need to be able to access that recording device. It needs to be accessed because they would need to retrieve the footage without necessarily having to go back into the house. If the end user wanted the device to be outside that person's property for a prolonged period of time, then you could potentially just put it inside a waterproof package such as a plastic bag or something of that nature which could then be placed behind a bush.

In figure 11, you will see a very basic device that you can find on most auction websites. It comes in the form of a little black box. It is a very small unit but big enough to contain the circuitry that we have discussed earlier in this section along with a SIM card and additional GSM based components that makes it possible for the device to make and receive calls. This allows the user to remotely monitor a conversation near where the device is planted, from anywhere in the world simply by calling the device. You simply insert the SIM card in which you have the telephone number for, this will activate or switch on the device. You then call the number, it answers and then you can monitor what's going on in that room. It is worth noting at this point that, the device does not ring or flash in any way. If the SIM card is a pay as you go, you put credit on it or if it's a contract SIM, you can run it on a contract.

Figure 11 - GSM Listening Device

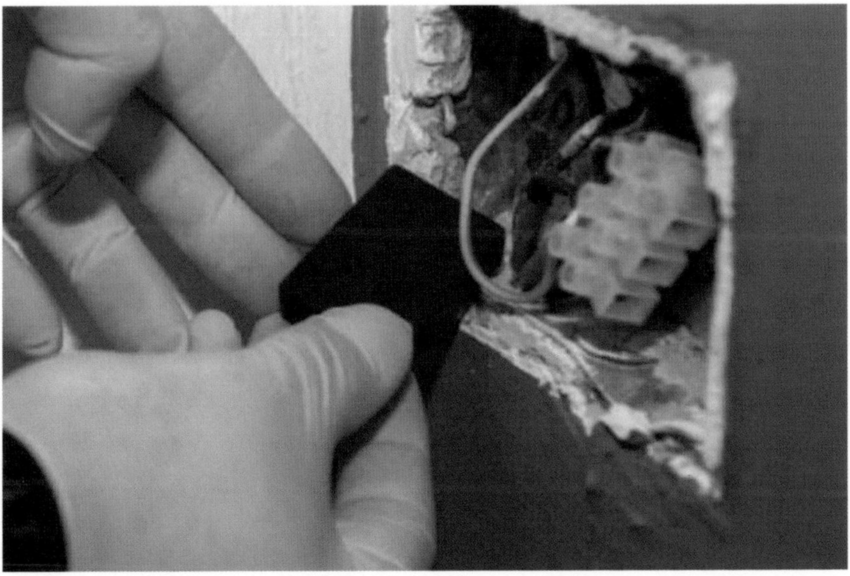

Figure 12 - GSM listening device found during a sweep

It can even be programmed by sending it a text message to call any number back when it detects noise. If I were to send it from my telephone number, then it would call my phone when it detects sound such as someone entering a room or someone slamming a cupboard shut or someone starts to talk then it will call my number back allowing me to monitor it. So if I store that telephone number in my phone as let's say 'bug in conference room', I can see that come up on my phone and I therefore know it is time to listen and it is of course live because it is a phone call.

Vehicle Tracking Devices

I would now like to discuss VTDs and their functions. The deployment and extraction of these devices will be covered later on in this book. Figure 13 is an image that was taken of an online panel in which you log into in order to access the vehicle tracking device data. Different manufacturers will have different platforms. This one is one that we have stuck with for a relatively long time as we consider it to be one that is reliable. I am now going to give you an overview as to its functions.

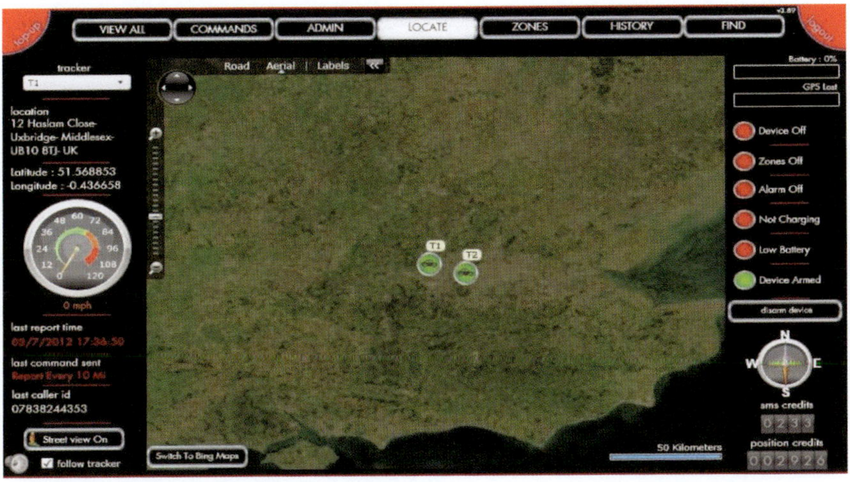

Figure 13 - Online Tracking Platform

On the image above, you will see a screenshot of a tracking platform which includes a satellite image that is populated by Google and has two vehicle tracking devices on it. To give you some background, at one point Vanquish® Investigation Services had somewhere in the region of 20 to 40 vehicle tracking devices deployed at any one time. This satellite image is of the South East of England with two vehicle tracking devices in and around the London area. On the upper left hand corner you will see the words 'Top Up'. The reason it says this is because they work using a mobile service meaning that the users had to top up the service with credits. Now if you take your eyes to the bottom right hand side of the image you will see SMS credits, it says two three three and then position credits to nine to six.

To give you further insight as to how that works, every time we want to send a command to the device, and I will explain what commands are in a moment, it would cost one SMS credit. The position credits relate to the amount of times the device tells the platform of its live location. In other words, every time it reports its position it takes off a 'position credit'. What would tend to happen over time is that, we would end up having a service for which we paid a set amount every month giving us unlimited position credits so that we didn't have to be too concerned about using all of the credits up.

Back to the top left hand side, if you look down slightly you will see the word 'tracker' and underneath that you will see 'T1'. That was a drop down menu which allowed us to select any vehicle tracking device and view its respective location and data. Underneath that it gives you the exact location which is usually the door number, street name and postcode. That address was not a specific address that related to an operation we had going on. You will see that the battery is actually dead and that just happened to be the last place where the vehicle was at the last time it reported its location.

Underneath the address it provides us with the longitude and latitude which is not very useful for most purposes. Underneath that, you will see that there is a speedometer which says that it was not driving at the time of the last report or that it was driving at '0 MILES PER HOUR'.

Below that, the last report time was on 03/07/2012 at 1736 hours and 50 seconds which, again, was the command received or it was the last time that someone sent a command to the device which, conversely, would have been the type of command that would have taken one SMS credit.

At some point, someone had sent a command which was to ask the device to report every 10 minutes. This could have been for a number of reasons. At the time of writing this book, they currently have the ability to report every 5 seconds with a number of variations all the way to reporting once every 24 hours. The reason you would have it report less frequently rather than more frequently, is to preserve battery life.

As your eyes glance below the battery level, you will see you can have the ability to use Street View which is quite useful as it allows you to explore the area to help you to identify whether the vehicle tracking device is at a residential property, a commercial property, what type of commercial property and so on.

Look back at the top of the image and you will see a number of buttons at the top. We will go left to right:
'View' is allowing you to look at all of the tracking devices that the panel has access to.

'Commands' will open up a drop list of options for you. One of which will be to reboot the device. If it is not responding properly you can ask it to reboot and then underneath that it will give you the options of report time. For example, every 5 seconds, every 10 seconds so on so forth.

The 'Admin' button will give you the option to change the icon image and other relevant aspects that manage the device settings.

‘Locate’ is just a quick option to enable you to locate the device relatively quickly.

‘Zones’ - This is quite an interesting one because it that allows you to draw an invisible circle in any part of this map which then gives you the ability to use it for two main purposes. We refer to these circles as ‘geofences’. The main function of a geofence is to notify you when the tracking device has either entered or exited an area/ zone. The geofence can be as little as one meter to one hundred miles in diameter, so it can cover a very large area if necessary. A geofence has a number of purposes. As an example in a security situation, if we had a principal (which is the person who is being protected by the security team), received a threat and we knew who the threat had been issued by, we could then deploy the tracking device onto that person's vehicle and monitor their movements whilst placing a geofence around the principal's property, maybe 10 miles which would then notify us if that vehicle entered that area. We would therefore have a 10 mile notice as to the fact that that individual has entered the zone and is potentially approaching the principal's address. The security team could then engage their pre-arranged ‘actions on drills’ to ensure that the principal is evacuated or secured.

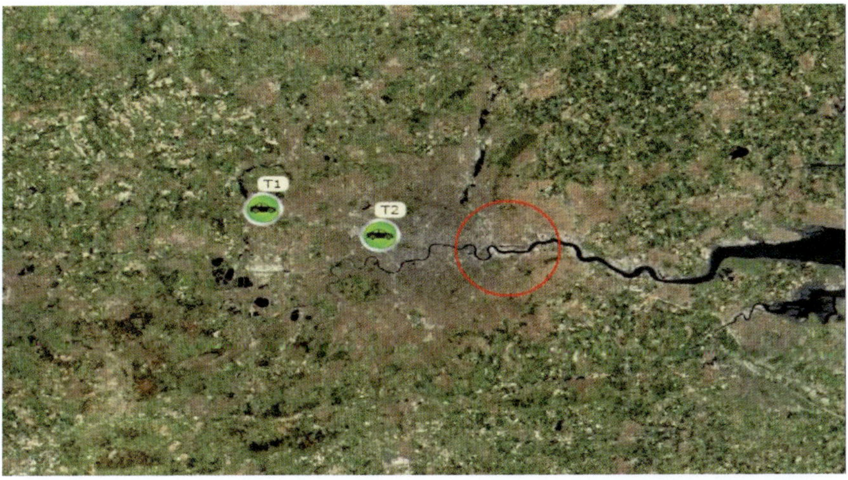

Figure 14 - A relatively large geofence surrounding City Airport in East London

The 'history' button will allow us to access a chronological list of every address that the vehicle tracker has visited. Bear in mind, however, that this will include all addresses close to where the vehicle had stopped. That will be inclusive of traffic lights stops etc which will have an impact on the report. But there is the option of checking a box that says 'stop and start only' and that will calculate all addresses that the tracker has stopped at for a period of 30 seconds or more. What it also does is it shows you on a map whether that be aerial or otherwise where the vehicle tracking has gone so you will almost see the road where the vehicle tracker has travelled. However if you are asking the vehicle tracking device to report every 10 minutes or longer, what you are going to see is a very grainy illustration of where the device has travelled. Although, it will show the stop and start locations, it will not necessarily show the roads because it would jump from one location to another every 10 minutes or for whatever time frame you have selected.

Underneath the 'find' option which is the same as locate you will see the battery level and the G.P.S. signal strength that indicates the amount of battery the device has left and the quality of the signal that it is receiving.

The 'armed' notification is just to let you know that the device is on and working.

Just to give you an idea as to the accuracy I have zoomed in a couple of times and in 2012, this was as far as you could zoom in. However now the devices are accurate up to 50 centimeters which means, based on the average size of a vehicle it will be very accurate indeed.

Covert Cameras

If you ever attend one of our surveillance courses in person, you will know that cameras can be incorporated into almost anything because we give out a number of examples on the course for you to look at to try and identify where the camera is actually hidden. This always proves quite a difficult task because they are so small nowadays and they `are becoming smaller and smaller as time goes on.
Some devices will record and some will send the data via a cellular signal or IP connection. So what does this mean?

Well, if it is a recording camera device that means you will have to extract the data or the footage in order for it to be useful to you or the person who wants to monitor that footage. This is very similar to the recording device discussed earlier. However, similar to listening devices, other camera devices will send a cellular signal which means they are transmitting the data live. Some of them, if they have an IP connection (internet protocol), may be hard wired which will make it slightly harder to find a signal. In fact, it will make it almost impossible to find a signal and you will have to use another search method which is covered later on in this book.

Wiretaps

Let me just say, you are very unlikely to find a wiretap. This is because they 'tap' into the wire of landline telephones which are not used as often as they once were and because we have developed other forms of communication such as emails, chat apps and so on. However, they play a huge part in the history of technical surveillance and we will therefore touch upon them now. Wiretaps have been around for as long as telephones have. In fact, in the 1860s before the modern telephone was even invented many state courts in the United States enacted statutes that prohibited anybody from listening in on what they used to refer to as "Telegraph communications".

Because landline telephones work using a bell wire, the only way for people to tap into that so to speak is to replicate the bell wire. In figure 15 you will see a wire splitter which can be

Figure 15 - Wiretap

found in most DIY stores. This product allows you to cut into an existing wire whilst placing a third party wire into it. The metal part in the centre will cut into both when the device is closed shut which will then allow the data to come from one wire, into your new wire where you can then monitor the communication through the new wire.

The photograph in figures 16 and 17 was taken a client's home address during a sweep. If you look closely as we zoom in you can see that there are what appears to be a couple of wire splitters in that unit. In this instance, the client decided to contact the police whom we assisted by providing them with a full report which could be later used as evidence.

Figure 16 - Suspected wiretap at client's HA during a sweep

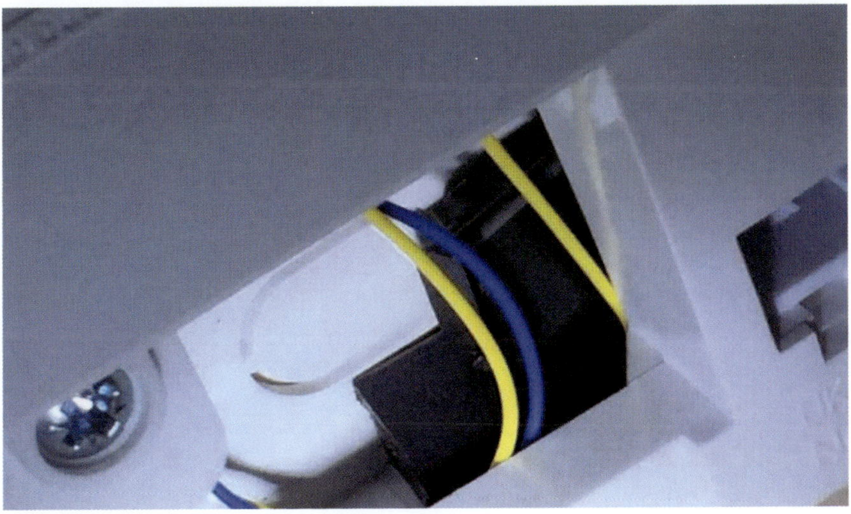

Figure 17 - Zoomed in image of figure 10

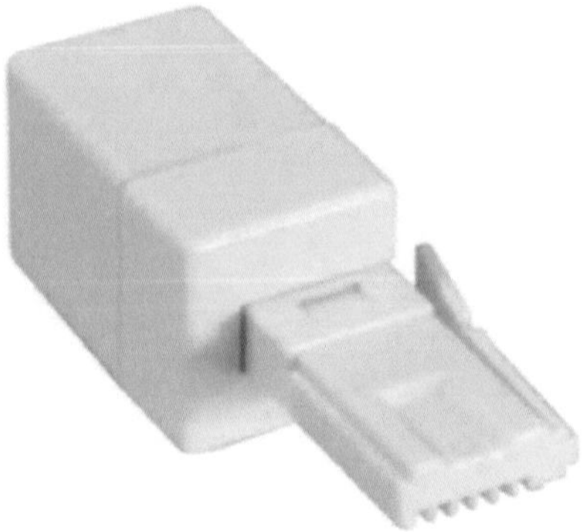

Figure 18 - Filter Unit

In figure 18 is something called a ‘filter unit’ which can be used to either record or transmit the data from telephone lines. In essence, the original telephone lead is plugged into this device before this device is plugged into the telephone socket. The downside to these products is that, they are quite noticeable to anyone who's living in the property.

VEHICLE TRACKING DEVICES
(DEPLOYMENT & DISCOVERY)

All vehicle tracking devices require a magnet in order for it to be applied to a vehicle. Some devices are already sealed in some form of material that encloses a magnet and others come with a waterproof pouch that has a magnet sewn into the material.

This section will look at how VTDs are applied to vehicles rather than how to find them because, it is not feasible to understand how to find them before you can understand how they are deployed. Therefore, the purpose of this is section of the book is to help you better understand how an operative would deploy them in an effort to help you identify where on a vehicle they can actually be found. The content that follows is from a five day Vanquish® training program for surveillance operatives who will learn as part of that course how to covertly deploy vehicle tracking devices.

Vehicle tracking devices can operate either as recording units or as live tracking units. This is very significant because TSCM operatives need to understand that not all vehicle tracking devices will necessarily emit a RF signal. If it is a live tracking unit, it will operate using GPS to facilitate its location monitoring function along with a 4G signal which it will emit to update some form of online platform or other information relay protocol. As you now know, GPS works via radio frequencies and as such, is detectable using the relevant RF detection device(s)/equipment.

But if it is a recording unit then it will only receive the signal from the GPS satellites and will store the information within it and therefore is more difficult to identify using RF detection.

Deployment

It is important to understand from the outset that vehicles have two sides which are commonly referred to as the 'off side' and the 'near side'. The off side is always the driver's side and the near side is always the passengers side. The theory goes that the near side is nearest to the pavement or the sidewalk, and the off side is the driver's side. By that standard, the 'sides' will change from country to country. In the UK, the right hand side of the vehicle would be the off side but in the United States, as an example, it would be the near side.

Figure 19 contains an image of a vehicle based in the UK because we drive on the right hand side and naturally the 'near side front' is at the top left hand corner of this image, with the 'off side front' being at the top right hand side and of course the 'near side rear' and the 'off side rear' being on their respective sides but to the rear of the vehicle.

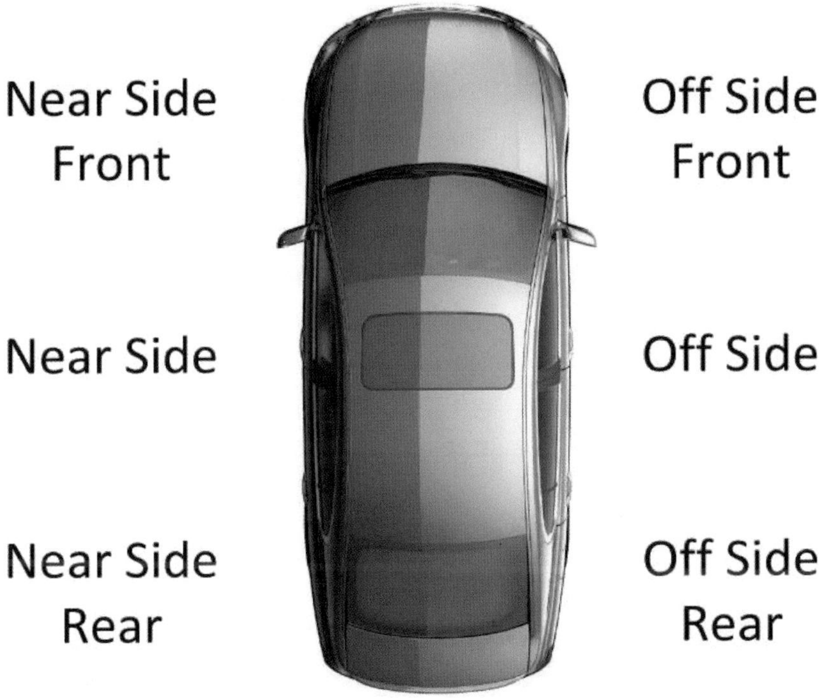

Figure 19 - Vehicle layout (right hand drive)

Safety First

Vehicle trackers are designed with one primary criteria in mind which is to track. The second priority in its design is durability. This is discussed during the deployment aspect of the training course (my 5 Day Advance Surveillance Course) as it is very important for those who will deploy these devices to understand that they need to have a very strong fixture to the vehicle, ensuring that it is not going to detach because some of them are very heavy and very strong. If they come off a high speed, they have the ability to cause a severe amount of devastating damage. Some of the devices are even designed specifically to resist intentional damage. One of the large tracking device manufacturers approached us a long time ago and actually gave me a demonstration on the device to show me how it was resistant up to 40 tons worth of pressure which is the equivalent of a lorry driving over it. Someone taking a hammer to it would not break it. It was actually waterproof as well it was sealed so that it could resist something in the region of 100 meters depth in terms of water submersion, so it was very robust. For that reason, those who deploy these devices have to be very conscious where on the vehicle the vehicle tracker is deployed ensuring that it is highly unlikely to fall off. They also have to bear in mind the integrity of the safety systems on the vehicle as well as the safety of our road users.

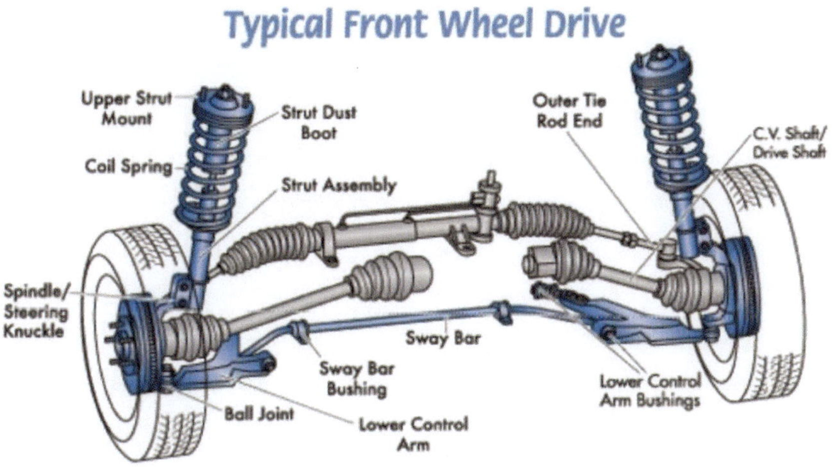

Figure 20 - Front wheel suspension (*Pinterest, 2019a*)

Figure 20 isolates a front wheel suspension assembly along with the drive shaft. The drive shaft comes from the gearbox and propels the vehicle so naturally they spin at a very high velocity meaning that a VTD should never be placed on them. Suspension arms (also referred to as wishbones) offer a very nice flat magnetic surface for a tracker to be deployed. Placing the device on top of the arm is often a good idea in some cases because of the benefit not only of the magnetic force, but also the force of gravity which will help reduce the likelihood of the vehicle tracking device coming off. However, the space between the drive shaft and the wishbone itself should be taken into consideration when deploying, owing to the simple fact that the device may be crushed if it is too close to the chassis or another part of the suspension system. I have pointed out another flat magnetic services that is available to someone deploying a device.

The most common area for a VTD to be deployed is the chassis. The chassis is often described as the 'skeleton' of the vehicle and is usually made from steel. As time goes on they are increasingly being manufactured out of aluminium presumably because the manufacturers want to reduce the weight and therefore harmful emissions. However, a majority of them are still made from steel and therefore offer a nice flat magnetic surface. You will also notice that the chassis has three sides to it. The outside, the underneath and the inside. Naturally the best place to deploy a device is on the inside with the magnets pointing outwards. It is an ideal location because if someone was to look under the vehicle, it slightly reduces the possibility of them seeing it. If you were to look underneath the vehicle that it was deployed on the underside of the chassis right here it would be quite obvious. The same goes for it being on the outside of the chassis (nearest to the outside of the vehicle). The chassis is usually isolated from any moving parts or sources of heat.

Figure 21 - Front wheel suspension

The device should not be deployed in one of the following areas:

That is anywhere near the engine, anywhere near the drive shaft or wheels or any other moving parts.

You should also ensure that you keep it away from the exhaust system because that will emit a huge amount of heat and potentially cause the battery within the device to explode.

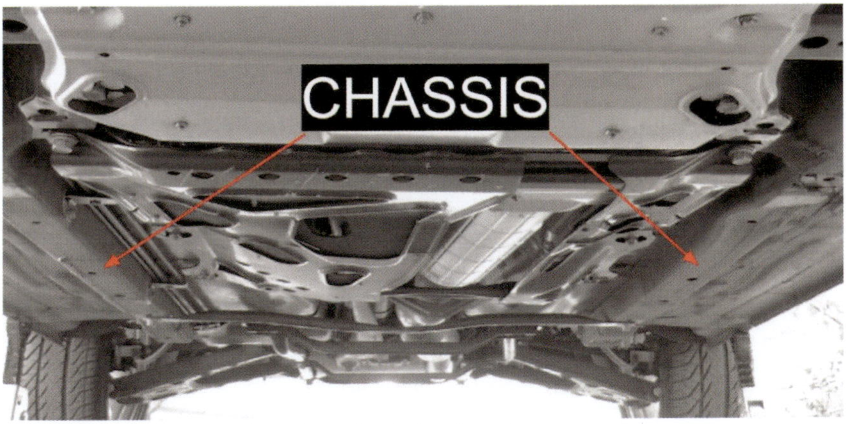

Figure 22 - Vehicle underside highlighting the chassis

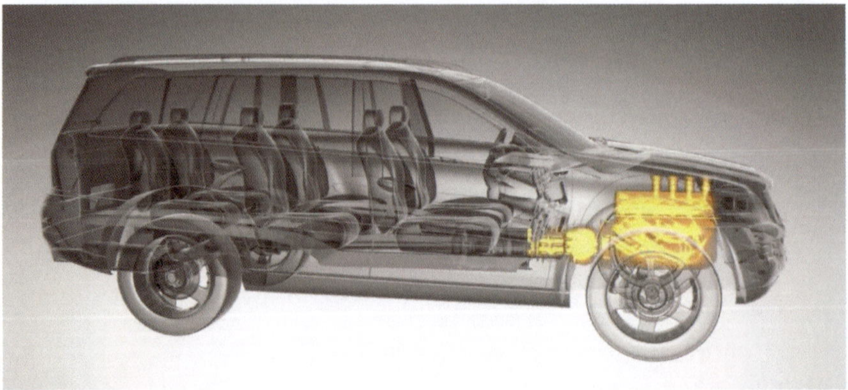

Figure 23 - Do not deploy near the engine or exhaust system

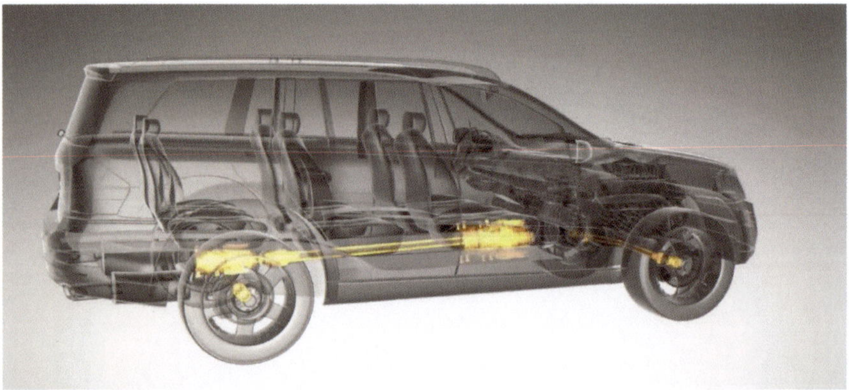

Figure 24 - Do not deploy near the drive shaft or other moving parts

Figure 25 - Moving parts includes the wheels

DEPLOYMENT

To provide some further insight, I have included the content from the course that teaches surveillance operatives how to deploy a VTD.

Before

Conduct a Dynamic Assessment - Once you have located the vehicle, you will need to check for the following:

No unwanted attention - The last thing you want is to be spotted by a neighbour who will inform the subject that someone has placed something underneath their vehicle.

Security - Are there any CCTV cameras that may be monitored live? Are there any "welcome lights" that will illuminate you and the vehicle as you approach it thus drawing unwanted attention to you? Conversely, there are a lot of CCTV cameras around but a very small percentage of them are monitored live.

Preparing yourself - It is advisable to wear surgical gloves whilst deploying a tracker. This will save you time because you will not have to clean your hands before driving off. Simply remove the gloves, and you are good to go.

Preparing the Device - Ensure that the device is switched on and fully charged. You can only do this by logging into the panel and checking.

Your Entry Route - How are you going to approach the vehicle? What will draw the least amount of unwanted attention?

During

Avoid Touching the Vehicle - Whilst deploying the device, it is best that you avoid touching the outside/ body of the vehicle as there is a risk of you leaving a mark on it or even worst, damaging the body itself. This is overlooked massively by most operatives whilst deploying the device. Imagine coming out to your vehicle in the morning and seeing finger marks all over the outside of it had you not cleaned it. It would highlight to you that it had been touched.

Best Location - Find the best possible place to deploy the device. This should ideally be done in less than 5 seconds.

Deploy the Device - Once you have located the best place for it, put the device on ensuring that is has a good magnetic connection and is not likely to fall off once the vehicle is mobile.

After

Leave the Area - Go to a location where you can take the time to confirm the deployment.

The remaining content is commercially sensitive and can only be disclosed during a training course.

A summary things to consider:

- You should now have a good understanding as to where on a vehicle a VTD will be deployed and therefore, discoverable.
- Vehicle tracking devices can be very heavy and robust. They should, therefore, be deployed somewhere that offers a good magnetic connection.
- They need to be in a position that is not easily seen from the outside of the vehicle or from someone looking at the vehicle from a generic point of view.
- Some vehicle trackers do emit a signal.
- Others only receive a signal and store the data within therefore only some devices can be found conducting a radio frequency detection based search.

MOBILE PHONE MONITORING

This section will look into what is probably one of the more common forms of technical surveillance. It is an interesting topic for many reasons, not least because of the way in which covert monitoring software is installed/ applied. In the private sector, bearing in mind the common restriction of funds available, there is only usually only one way to install such software which is to physically have access to the subject device. That said, it could be argued that technology will make it easier for the general public to remotely and covertly install software as time goes on. I would argue however, that the sophistication of the default security settings within devices, relevant legislation and other factors will prevent this from becoming a reality. Whilst the knowledge may become more widely available, the deterrent will also do so.

The sections to follow form part of the training course in which we discuss mobile phone monitoring to raise awareness of the available products that are available to the public. We specifically concentrate on one, reasonably cheap product that has a huge range of capabilities. Firstly, we will look at why monitoring software is probably the more common form of covert mobile phone monitoring.

There are three main ways in the which a mobile cellular device can be monitored.

A modern smartphone will record and save certain data (text messages, emails, call list etc).
All data from the device (other than the content of the phone calls themselves) will be registered with the service provider. This includes SMS messages, call logs and so on.

In the UK, it is illegal to record a phone call without making both parties aware. This, of course does not prevent it from happening.

Acquiring call logs, SMS and other sensitive data that is legally protected under the Data Protection Act 1998 in the UK (and similar acts in other countries/ states), is not unheard of. Simply by having the subject telephone number, the right contacts and the funds available you can potentially and unlawfully acquire the owner's full address, payment details call logs, SMS logs and more. This is not only illegal but completely useless to anyone who wishes to use the intelligence for legal purposes as it will not be admissible in court. Anyone who chooses to record a phone call without permission will face similar issues.

Below you will see a list of the functions of the reasonably cheap product mentioned earlier:

- Monitor Calls
- Incoming Calls Restriction
- Sent / Received SMS
- Incoming / Outgoing E-mails
- Current GPS Location
- Browsing History
- Website Bookmarks
- Blocking Websites
- Calendar
- Activities
- Contacts
- Skype
- WhatsApp
- iMessage
- Social Networking
- Viber
- Bugging
- Installed Applications
- Application blocking
- Keylogger
- Photos/ Videos
- Device Wipeout
- Device Locking
- Additional Device Info
- Control Panel
- Comprehensive Reports

Once the software has been successfully installed, all of the above is monitored from anywhere in the world via an online platform as long as the subject device has an internet (3G, 4G or WiFi) connection. Although the software is often installed as an app, it usually disappears and integrates into the operating system so that it can function covertly without alerting the device user.

The process in which it is established, whether or not such software is installed on a device is consistently changing as technology evolves and varies from brand to brand. In an effort to maintain the relevance of this book, I will not go through the current procedures. The best option, should you come across such a scenario of suspecting that a mobile device is being monitored, would be to have the device sent to a technician for them to forensically examine.

Summary

Mobile phone monitoring software is rarely installed remotely because of the implications involved. These implications are mainly financial. Because of this, the person who installs the software would need to have physical access to the phone along with any passcodes associated with it.

It is possible for criminals to gain access to a phone user's data by going through a corrupt employee of the service provider.

Legislation relating to the monitoring of telephone communication varies from country to country.

Because of the constant evolution of technology and the speedy progression of mobile phone's operating systems, it is strongly recommended that a professional technical forensic operative carries out the relevant checks to determine whether or not malicious monitoring software has been installed on any given device.

PC, LAPTOP AND TABLET MONITORING

Spy software or 'spyware', is a malicious program that covertly runs on PCs, laptops or tablets. It can on occasions be installed remotely but is more commonly installed directly onto the device.

Keystroke software essentially monitors everything that the subject user enters into their device. This will include websites, usernames, passwords, bank details, email content the list goes on. The most basic software is arguably the most effective as it is small in terms of the amount of disk space it requires to operate and therefore harder for security software packages to detect.

In 2012, Vanquish incorporated a software development company which produced a very basic keylogging product which is a useful and relevant example. The target market was corporate clients enabling them to monitor their employees' activities. It was also useful for parents who had concerns about their children's use of the devices. The data received back by the end user was considered very 'raw' and did take some time to interpret. This was one of the major downfalls of the product.

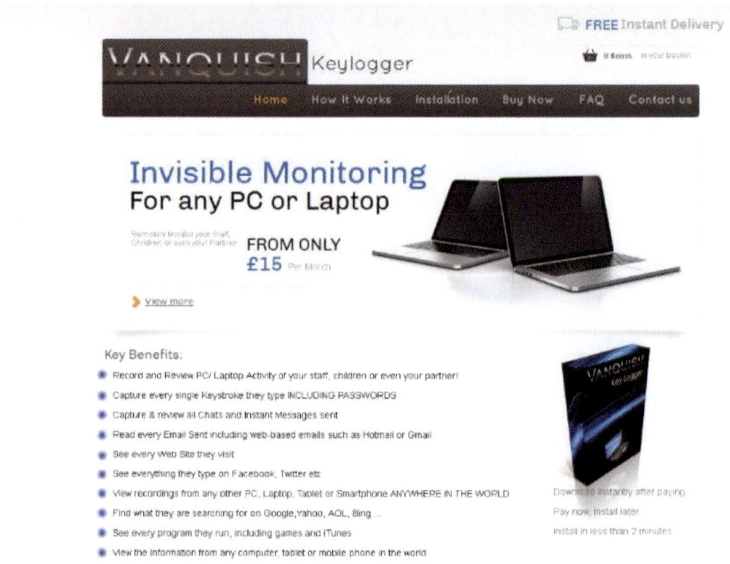

Figure 27 - V Keylogger website from 2013

Below is an example of raw data that could have been received by an end user after installing the software onto a subject device:

```
16/08/2012@1158 - www.facebook.comenter
16/08/2012@1158 - myexampleusername@gmail.comtab
16/08/2012@1158 - myfakepasswordenter
```

The time and date are highlighted on the left and the keystrokes on the right. Observe how it states ‘enter’ and ‘tab' along with the useful, informative data. This is because it literally recorded and reported back every keystroke to the end user. The 'tab' button is used to jump from one input field to another. In this example, the subject has entered their Facebook username which is their email address, pressed tab to move onto the password field, entered their password and hit 'enter' to log into the site. As basic and raw as it was, you can see how effective it could be.

Process for manual installation (not remote):

- The installer (end user) will need physical access to the device as well as knowing the password.
- When purchased, the end user will have received an email containing a download link along with a licence key. The licence key is to ensure that the end user only uses the product for the amount of devices that they have paid for.
- Once access to the PC, laptop or tablet has been acquired, they will need to then access their email account. This is only possible if they are using an accessible host such as Gmail or Hotmail.
- In the email they received after purchasing the software, they will have a link to which they can click and download onto the subject device.
- Once downloaded they will need to enter the licence key in order for it to start installing.

- As part of the installation process, the end user will be prompted to enter an email address. This is where all of the data will be sent to.
- Once installation is complete, the software/ app will disappear and disguise itself within the operating system.
- The software will then begin to send reports every set amount of time (20 minutes or so). Some products have an online platform for the end user to visit and view the data there.
- The end user should log out of their email account and delete the browsing history to cover their tracks.

The software was also available on a memory stick which alleviated the requirement to log into an email account whilst on the subject device.

Up until around 2016, we used to teach the candidates who attended the Vanquish® TSCM course how to check for spyware. This has now changed owing to the constant development of operating systems, different and new manufacturers along with a number of other factors. We now advise clients that a specialist needs to check the items as it is indeed a specialist field that falls out of the scope of this book.

Summary

PC and laptop monitoring software is rarely installed remotely because of the implications involved. These implications are mainly financial. Because of this, the person who installs the software would need to have physical access to the device along with any passcodes associated with it.

Legislation relating to the covert monitoring of such devices varies from country to country.

Because of the constant evolution of technology and the speedy progression of PCs, laptops and tablets and their operating systems, it is strongly recommended that a professional technical forensic operative carries out the relevant checks to determine whether or not malicious monitoring software has been installed on any given device.

DSLR PHOTOGRAPHY

Here's some steps for learning how to use that new DSLR that we'll cover in this chapter.

1. Master Shooting modes (including priority modes and full manual)
2. Understand ISO
3. Learn the 'exposure triangle'
4. Master Metering including exposure compensation
5. Learn About Focussing
6. Understand file size/types
7. Learn about White balance

There's lots to learn if you want to get the most from your DSLR but let's start by digging into each of these topics.

Figure 28 - A selection of DSLR cameras

1. Master Shooting Modes

The best place to start is with shooting modes. The shooting modes will most likely be found on a dial labelled with 'auto, Av, Tv, P, M' and maybe more. Selecting a shooting mode will determine how your camera behaves when you press the shutter, for example, when 'auto' is selected, the camera will determine everything to do with the exposure, including the aperture and shutter speed. The other modes, 'Av, Tv, P, M', are there to give you control:

Figure 29

How to Use a DSLR - Shooting Modes Dial

Don't worry if your mode dial looks a little different; different manufacturers use different abbreviations for the shooting modes. Your mode dial may have the letters 'A, S, P, M' (instead of Av, Tv, P, M), yet they all function in the same way.

Below, I have given each abbreviation for the given mode.

Aperture Priority (Av or A)

Aperture priority can be thought of as a 'semi-automatic' shooting mode. When this is selected, you as the photographer set the aperture and the camera will automatically select the shutter speed. So what is aperture and when would you want to control it?

The aperture is the size of the opening in the lens through which light is allowed to pass whenever the shutter is opened – the larger the aperture, the more light passes through.

The aperture is measured in 'f-stops' and is usually displayed using an 'f-number', e.g. f/2.0, f/2.8, f/4.0, f/5.6, f/8.0 etc, which is a ratio of focal length over diameter of the opening. Therefore, a larger aperture (a wider opening) has a smaller f-number (e.g. f/2.0) and smaller aperture (a narrower opening) has a larger f-number (e.g. f/22). Reducing the aperture by one whole f-stop, e.g. f/2.0 to f2/8 or f/5.6 to f/8.0, halves the amount of light entering the camera.

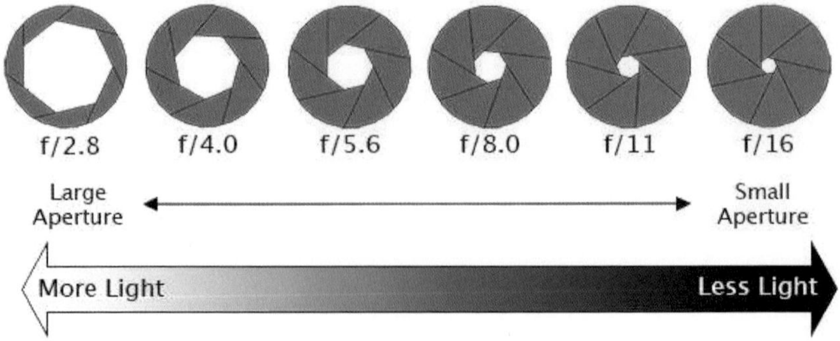

Figure 14 - Our area of interest

How to Use a DSLR Aperture illustration

Aperture is one of the most important aspects of photography as it directly influences the depth of field – that is, the amount of an image that is in focus. A large depth of field (achieved by using a small aperture (large f-number)) would mean that a large distance within the scene is in focus, such as the foreground to the background of the landscape below.

Figure 31 -

An aperture of f/13 was used here to give a large depth of field, ensuring that the whole image, from the foreground grasses to the background mountains. was sharp

Whereas a shallow depth of field (achieved by using a large aperture (small f-number)) would produce an image where only the subject is in sharp focus, but the background is soft and out of focus. This is often used when shooting portraiture or wildlife, such as the image below, to isolate the subject from the background:

Figure 32 -

large aperture
A large aperture of f/4.5 was used to capture this water vole, against a soft, out of focus background

So when using aperture priority, you can get complete control over your depth of field, whilst the camera takes care of the rest.

Shutter Priority (Tv or S)

Similarly to aperture priority, this is another 'semi-automatic' shooting mode, though in this instance, you as the photographer set the shutter speed and the camera will take care of the aperture. The shutter speed, measured in seconds (or more often fractions of a second), is the amount of time the shutter stays open when taking a photograph. The longer the shutter stays open, the more light passes through to the sensor to be captured.

You would select a short shutter speed if you wanted to freeze a fast moving subject, such as shooting sports, action or wildlife, for example:

Figure 33 - fast shutter speed

A very fast shutter speed of 1/4000th sec was used to freeze the motion of this grouse in flight

You would use a long shutter speed if you wanted to blur a moving subject, for example water rushing over a waterfall (slower shutter speeds will require you to put the camera on a tripod to ensure the camera is held steady whilst the shutter is open):

Figure 34 -

Slow Shutter Speed

To capture the motion of the waves, and render the water with a soft, milky texture, a shutter speed of 6 seconds was used here

So whilst you worry about what shutter speed you need for a given photograph, the camera will determine the appropriate aperture required to give the correct exposure.

Aperture and shutter priority shooting modes may be semi-automatic, meaning that some may deride their use because they're not fully manual, however they are incredibly useful modes to shoot in that can give you enough creative control to capture scenes as you envisage them.

Program (P)

Program mode is almost a halfway house between the semi automatic modes of aperture/shutter priority and full manual control. In program mode, you are able to set either the aperture or shutter speed, and the camera will maintain the correct exposure by adjusting the other one accordingly, i.e. as you change the aperture, the shutter speed will automatically change, and vice versa. This gives you additional freedom that using either aperture priority or shutter priority cannot give without switching between shooting modes.

Manual (M)

Manual mode is exactly what it sounds like, you are given full control over the exposure determination, setting both the aperture and shutter speed yourself. There will be an exposure indicator either within the viewfinder or on the screen that will tell you how under/over exposed the image will be, however, you are left to change the shutter speed and aperture yourself to ensure you achieve the correct exposure.

Practically Speaking: as a first step to taking your camera off 'auto', aperture priority and shutter priority modes offer two very simple ways to start to understand how the different setting impact your images and are a perfect starting place for learning how to use your camera more creatively.

2. Understand ISO

ISO is a measure of how sensitive the sensor of your camera is to light. The term originated in film photography, where film of different sensitivities could be used depending on the shooting conditions, and it is no different in digital photography. The ISO sensitivity is represented numerically from ISO 100 (low sensitivity) up to ISO 6400 (high sensitivity) and beyond, and controls the amount of light required by the sensor to achieve a given exposure. At 'low' sensitivities, more light is required to achieve a given exposure compared to high sensitivities where less light is required to achieve the same exposure. To understand this, let's look at two different situations:

Low ISO numbers

If shooting outside, on a bright sunny day there is a lot of available light that will hit the sensor during an exposure, meaning that the sensor does not need to be very sensitive in order to achieve a correct exposure. Therefore, you could use a low ISO number, such as ISO 100 or 200. This will give you images of the highest quality, with very little grain (or noise).

Figure 35 - DSLR - Low ISO Taken at ISO 100, the image does not show signs of noise (even when looking at the 100% crop (right)

High ISO numbers

If shooting in low light conditions, such as inside a dark cathedral or museum for example, there is not much light available for your camera sensor. A high ISO number, such as ISO 3200, will increase the sensitivity of the sensor, effectively multiplying the small amount of available light to give you a correctly exposed image. This multiplication effect comes with a side effect of increased noise on the image, which looks like a fine grain, reducing the overall image quality. The noise will be most pronounced in the darker/shadow regions.

Figure 36 -

High ISO

This image was taken as the sun was going down, meaning there was not much ambient light. Therefore, this was shot with ISO4000, however you can see very obvious noise in the 100% crop (right)

Practically Speaking: you want to keep the ISO as low as possible, as the lower the ISO, the less noise and the higher the quality of the resulting image. Outside on a sunny day, select ISO200 and see how it goes. If it clouds over, maybe select an ISO between 400-800. If you move indoors, consider an ISO of around 1600 or above (these are approximate starting points).

Most digital SLRs now have an 'auto-ISO' function, where the camera sets the ISO depending upon the amount of light in which you are shooting, keeping it as low as possible. Auto-ISO is a very useful tool when starting out with your camera, as it is allows you to define an upper limit i.e. where the images become too noisy such as ISO1600 or 3200, and then forget about it until situations where you specifically want to override the automatic setting, for example if taking landscape images using a tripod, you can afford to use the lowest ISO possible.

3. Learn the 'Exposure Triangle'

It's important to note that aperture, shutter speed and ISO are all part of the 'exposure triangle'. They all control either the amount of light entering the camera (aperture, shutter speed) or the amount of light required by the camera (ISO) for a given exposure.

Therefore, they are all linked, and understanding the relationship between them is crucial to being able to take control of your camera.

A change in one of the settings will impact the other two. For example, considering a theoretical exposure of ISO400, f/8.0, 1/10th second. If you wanted to reduce the depth of field, and decided to use an aperture of f/4.0, you would be increasing the size of the aperture by two whole f/stops, therefore increasing the amount of light entering the camera by a factor of 4 (i.e. increasing by a factor of 2, twice). Therefore, to balance the exposure, you could do the following:

- Situation 1: Reduce the shutter speed by a factor of 4, i.e. to 1/40th second.
- Situation 2: Reduce the ISO by a factor of 4, i.e. to ISO100
- Situation 3: A combination of the above, shutter speed by a factor of 2 (to 1/20th second) AND reduce the ISO bv a factor of 2 (to ISO200).

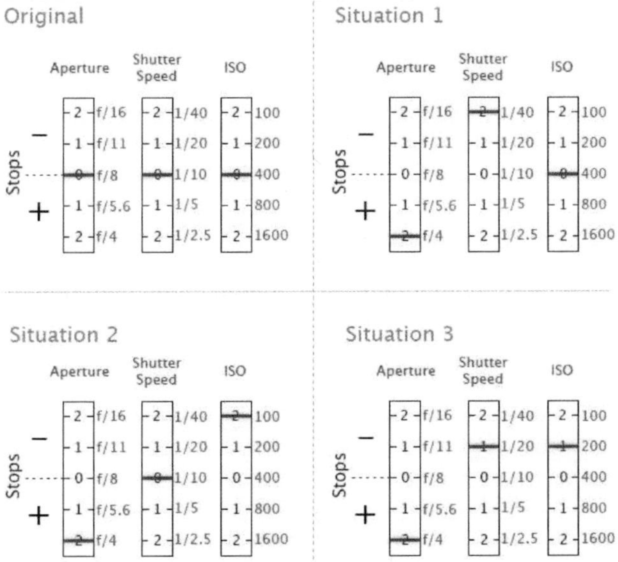

Figure 37 - Aperture, shutter speed and ISO are all factors that influence your exposure, and are all linked. It's just a case of balancing the books!

They all have the net effect of reducing the amount of light by a factor of 4, countering the change in aperture. It's just a case of understanding that they are all linked, and so changing one setting, will cause a change in another.

Using a combination of the semi-automatic shooting modes and auto-ISO would mean you won't necessarily need to think about adjusting your exposure in such a way initially, however understanding the relationship that ISO or aperture has with shutter speed, and knowing the practical implications is a big step in mastering your DSLR .

4. Master Metering

Throughout all of the above discussion, I have said that the camera calculates the exposure depending on the amount of available light, but what is it actually doing?

When taking a photograph, using any form of automatic exposure calculation (e.g. aperture priority mode, shutter priority mode, auto-ISO etc) the camera always tries to calculate an 'average' exposure. It will asses the entire scene, both light and dark areas, and determine the exposure so that all of the tones within the entire image average to 18% grey – called the 'middle' grey.

This is known as metering, and it is the reason that if you point your camera at a bright white scene, such as after it has snowed, and take a photograph the resulting image will always appear darker than you or I see it. Similarly, if you point your camera at a really dark scene, such as a low-lit room, and take a photograph the resulting image will always be brighter than you or I see it.

The scene is always being averaged by the camera and most of the time that results in the image appearing to be correctly exposed. However, you can control what areas of the scene are being assessed by the camera in order to influence the way in which the exposure is metered.

Generally, there are three metering modes that you can choose from:

Average – The camera will assess the tones across the entire image form corner to corner, and expose the scene to 18% grey from that assessment.

Centre-weighted – The camera weights the exposure reading for the area in the centre of the viewfinder that can total up to approximately 80% of the scene, ignoring the extreme corners of the image.

Spot metering – The camera will use a very small area of the scene, typically a small circle in the centre of the viewfinder that totals approximately 5% of the viewfinder area. It will make the assessment of dark/light tones in this area and expose the entire scene to 18% grey, from that assessment.

Practically speaking: when starting out with your camera, either average or centre weighted metering are a good starting point. They will both provide a fairly consistent measure of the exposure required and, if you select one mode and stick with it, you will soon begin to understand when a scene will be under exposed (i.e. too dark) or over exposed (i.e. to light) compared to how you see it with your own eyes.

But what can you do if a scene is under/over exposed? That is where exposure compensation comes in.

Exposure Compensation

Generally found on a small +/- button near the shutter, this is one of the most useful functions to learn how to use. It allows you to either increase or decrease the cameras default meter reading to account for the actual brightness of a scene.

Figure 38 - DSLR - Low ISO Taken at ISO 100, the image does not show signs of noise (even when looking at the 100% crop (right)

If a scene contains primarily bright tones and is being rendered too dark, for example, a bright white snow scene (that will typically be reduced to 18% grey by the default metering system), you can apply positive exposure compensation to let the camera know that the scene should be lighter than middle grey.

Figure 39 -

A spring lamb leaping in front of a snowy hillside. Left: Straight out of camera, with the snow caught as grey. Right: With +2 stops exposure compensation (added in post processing). The bright snowy background caused my camera to underexpose this scene by nearly two stops, which could have been corrected by exposure compensation in camera

Conversely, if a scene contains primarily dark tones and is being rendered too light, for example, a dark night scene (that will typically be increased to 18% grey by the default metering system), you can apply negative exposure compensation to let the camera know that the scene should be darker than middle grey.

5. Learn About Focussing

Regardless of what shooting mode you are using, or what ISO you define, the chances are there will be a subject of your image that you want to have in focus. If that focus is not achieved, the image will not be what you wanted.

Autofocus modes

DSLRs come with a range of autofocus modes, however, for simplicity, the two that are most important to understand are AF-S and AF-C

AF-S – autofocus-single. This is best used when taking photos of stationary subjects such as portraits of people, landscapes, buildings etc. When you half-press the shutter, the focus will be acquired and locked on that point for as long as you hold the button down. If you want to change to focus, you need to release the button, recompose and then re-half-press.

AF-C – autofocus-continuous. This is best used when taking photos of action or moving subjects such as sports and wildlife. When you half-press the shutter, focus will be acquired and locked on to a given subject. When that subject moves, the focus will adjust with it, refocusing all of the time until the photograph is taken.

(These modes are not to be confused with the AF/MF switches on the lens, where AF stands for autofocus and MF stands for manual focus. That switch is an override for if you want to manually focus your lens. If you want to make use of the autofocus modes discussed above, ensure the lens is set to AF).

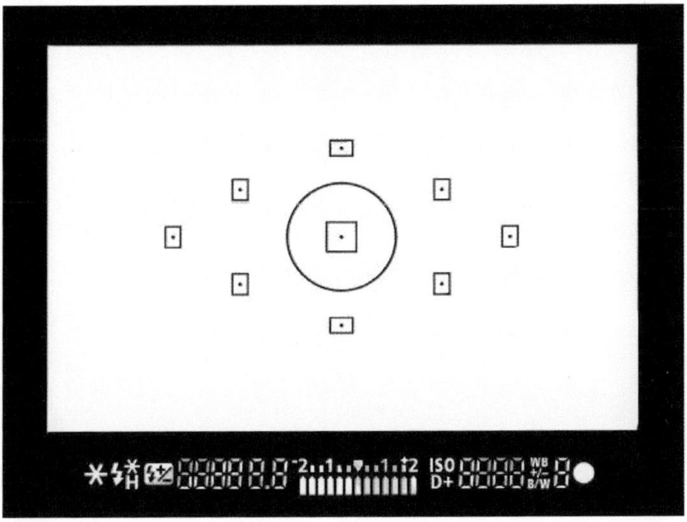

Figure 40 -

New DSLRs can come with over 50 focus points and the temptation is to leave it on fully automatic focus point selection, with the thinking that the camera will be able to select the correct focus point. However, only you know what you want to focus on, and there is no better way than ensuring the correct subject is in focus than by using one focus point, and placing that focus point over the subject.

If you select a single focus point, you should be able to change which point is active fairly easily either by using directional buttons one of the dials. If you select a focus point that is on your desired subject, you will ensure that the camera focuses where you want it to. After a small amount of practice, you will soon get into the habit of being able to change the focus point without taking the camera away from your eye.

Practically speaking: Initially, set your camera to use a single focus point (your camera manual should tell you how to do this). This way, you will be able to choose what you are focussing on, ensuring that the subject you want to capture is in focus. Once you are familiar with the basic focussing modes and focus point selection, you can then explore the more advanced modes that your camera may offer

6. Understand File Size and Types

You will have the option to be able to change the size of the images that your camera records, and in which file type. You want to set the file size to the largest possible (whether it is 'large' or 'fine' or 'super fine') to ensure that you are making the most of the mega pixels that you have just invested in.

You will also have the option of choosing whether to record the images as 'raw' or 'jpeg' file type. A raw file is uncompressed, and so contains a lot of image data that allows for a lot of flexibility during post-processing (i.e. on your computer) but also comes with additional complications such as the need to 'process' every file using dedicated editing software and a larger file size. A jpeg is a compressed file type, that is automatically processed by the camera. They will be 'print ready' straight out of the camera, and are much smaller files, meaning you can fit more images per memory card.

Practically speaking: When starting out with your camera, using jpeg is the most straight forward. It will enable you to get the best results whilst you learn the basics or your camera before complicating matters with post-processing of raw files.

7. Learn about white balance

If shooting in jpeg, as recommended above, you will need to make sure you set your white balance before taking a picture. The white balance can significantly impact colour tone of your photographs. You may have noticed that sometimes your images have a blueish tone to them or, in others, everything looks very orange. This is to do with the white balance and, whilst you can make some adjustments to the image on your computer, it is much simpler if you get it right up-front.

Different light sources (such as the sun, light bulbs, fluorescent strips etc) emit light of different wavelengths, and therefore colours, which can be described by what is known as colour temperature. Light from a candle, or from the sun during sunrise/sunset, is very warm, and contains a lot of red/orange wavelengths; whereas light from a fluorescent strip is much cooler, containing a lot of blue wavelengths. This coloured light is reflected off of surfaces, but our brain in clever enough to recognise this and automatically counter the effect, meaning that we still see a white surface as a white surface. However, your camera is not that intelligent, and unless told otherwise, will record the orange or blue tones giving the colour cast to your images.

Figure 41 -

Left: The image captured using auto white balance has a heavy yellow tone from the artificial street lighting. Right: the same image, corrected for a 'Tungsten' white balance, giving the cooler tones on the stone work, and the bluer sky

As the colour temperature of different light sources is well known, there are a number of presets built into your camera that help to overcome the different colours of light in different situations – cooling the warm light, and warming the cool light – all in the cause of trying to capture the colours of the scene accurately. The 'auto' feature (auto WB or AWB) will attempt to predict the colour of the light by detecting the predominant colour of the scene and then countering it, however it may not necessarily make a correct decision, leaving you with inaccurate colours. Therefore it is best to set the colour balance before you take your image and just to make sure (note: the above image was a raw file giving me a lot of latitude for white balance correction. Jpeg files are not as susceptible to white balance adjustments, meaning the white balance correction needs to be made before the image is taken):

Daylight – To be used on clear sunny days. Bright sunlight, on a clear day is as near to neutral light that we generally get

Cloudy – To be used when shooting on a cloudy day. Adds warm tones to daylight images.

Shade – To be used if shooting in the shade, as shaded areas generally produce cooler, bluer images, so need warming up.

Tungsten – Used for shooting indoors, under incandescent light bulbs, or under street lights, to cool down the yellow tones.

Fluorescent – Compensates for the green/blue tones of fluorescent light strips when shooting indoors.

Flash – the flash will add a cool blue cast to the image, so used to add some warmth.

Practically speaking: avoid auto white balance and set the white balance manually. Generally, you will be able to look up at the sky and see what kind of day it is, and determine the colour

balance required pretty easily. If you move indoors, just check the lighting that you are shooting under, and again select the appropriate white balance. It will soon become second nature to set it as you take your camera out of the bag.

Summary

So that is an overview of the settings you will encounter when you want to take the leap and take your camera off 'Auto'. You don't necessarily need to consider them all straight away, but exploring and understanding the effect of each setting will soon have you in complete control of your camera. The biggest step, that will give you the most noticeable difference in the feeling of control and direct influence on creative results, will be to start using the 'aperture priority' or 'shutter priority' shooting modes and once you are familiar with those, you can start thinking about exploring further. Soon enough, you will no longer think of your camera as a mysterious black box, but understand how to achieve the photographic results that you bought it for in the first place

(*digital-photography-school.com, 2019*)

COMMUNICATIONS

Two-Way Radios – Radios can be used covertly by bluetooth connected earpieces. This means that there are no wires to your ear and no wires to your hand for a microphone, just a Bluetooth adapter on the radio itself which enables the user to have a wireless earpiece and microphone. They are slightly expensive but are very useful. Below is an image of a popular two way radio used by security companies worldwide.

Figure 42 - A Motorola CP040 radio

PTT

When operating the PTT button, it is important you follow procedure or else you will not send your full message. The procedure is as follows:

P – Push

P – Pause

S – Speak

P – Pause

R – Release

This stops the user from pressing and talking too early or releasing the button before he/ she has finished speaking.

Channel Selector

All radios have channels. In order for a group of radios to work together they must be on the same channel. For obvious reasons, this should be checked prior to the team deploying.

The sound test buttons

These are a bit of a red herring in the sense that no one really ever seems to know what they are for. I have only used them to test the sound whilst wearing an earpiece. So, press them in whilst adjusting the volume knob.

Voice Over Net Procedures

It is important for any surveillance operative to know and understand radio protocols. Radio communications can be used in large surveillance teams so the last thing you want is to say something stupid whilst everyone is listening. Firstly you need to be familiar with the phonetic alphabet:

A - Alpha	N - November
B - Bravo	O - Oscar
C - Charlie	P - Papa
D - Delta	Q - Quebec
E - Echo	R - Romeo
F - Fox-Trot	S - Sierra
G - Golf	T - Tango
H - Hotel	U - Uniform
I - India	V - Victor
J - Juliet	W - Whisky
K - Kilo	X - X-ray
L - Lima	Y - Yankee
M - Mike	Z - Zulu

With regards to numbers, refer to 0 as zero not the letter 'O'. When you mention a number such as 23 spell it out as "two three" not "twenty three".

Here are some keywords that are used when conversing using two way radios:

Negative – No

Loud and Clear – I can hear you. You may also hear people say "Lima Charlie", which are the respective word in the phonetic alphabet.

Over – I have finished talking and I am listening for your reply.

Out – I have finished talking to you and do not expect a reply. DO NOT SAY “over and out”. That is a huge misconception that is only used in films.

Roger – (also **roger that**) I understand what you said; ok; all right.

Copy - An alternative to “roger”.

Send – Go Ahead. Short for “Send your message”.

Say Again – or Go Again, repeat; Please repeat your last message.

Roger So Far – Confirm you have received and understood the contents of my transmission so far. This is used during Long Message Procedure (Messages lasting over 20 seconds).

Standby or **Wait out** – Pause for the next transmission.

WillCo - I will comply.

Notice we use the word ‘negative’ but nothing for the opposite. Americans tend to say ‘Affirmative’. We tend to say ‘yes yes’ or ‘answer yes’. I don’t know why. Also, we combine the standard radio language with some of the jargon that we discussed at the beginning of the book. Here is an example of how conversation may go:

The surveillance operative has been given a code name (Alpha 10)

HQ: Hello alpha one zero, this is hotel Quebec, over.

Surveillance Operative: alpha one zero, send over.

HQ: what is your loc-stat, over.

Surveillance Operative: I am at the subject's HA, no movement from the subject yet, over.

HQ: Roger, out.

See how the surveillance operative's first response was "alpha one zero, send over". He was identifying himself as alpha one zero.

COVERT COMMS

Covert communications play a huge role in the outcome of a surveillance task. Operatives use a number of methods and resources to communicate with one another however, it is necessary at this point to clarify the definition of *covert communications*. At the time of writing this book, if you used the keywords 'covert radio communications', the shopping or image base results will show what is colloquially referred to as a "curly wurly'. These are the type of earpieces that are used by high profile close protection teams and there is nothing covert about them. If you were seen with this in your ear in central London whilst acting suspiciously on your surveillance operation, you would be stopped by police within minutes which would very

Figure 43 - A "Curly Wurly" Earpiece

likely lead to a compromise. Covert does not mean discreet, it means undercover and out of sight. It is formally defined as '*not openly acknowledged or displayed'.* Operatives are therefore encouraged to be mindful of this when seeking to purchase and utilise such equipment.

If two way radios were the selected method of communication then the earpieces used would be the type that operate using a bluetooth connection to the handheld unit. The user pushes a button (often placed in their pocket) to engage the PTT (push to

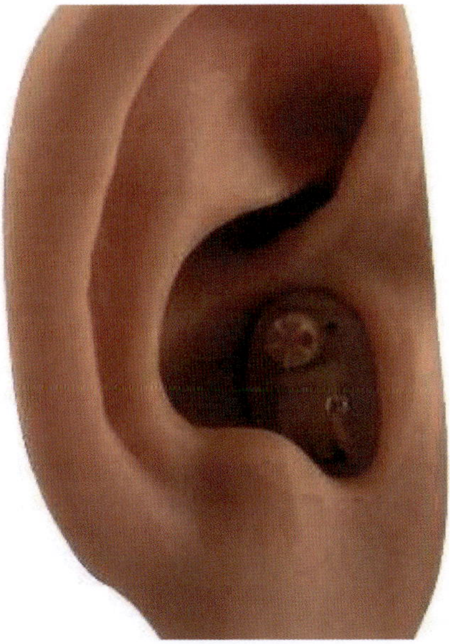
Figure 44 - A covert bluetooth earpiece

talk) button allowing them to speak into a microphone that is located underneath their clothing, preferably without pushing their chin towards their chest making it quite obvious that they are speaking into a hidden mic.

Hand Signals – This is a popular choice and something that we do on the course when we deploy the teams out on their practical live surveillance operations. Hand signals are used by surveillance teams to quickly pass on information between one another. Sometimes there is not enough time to get a mobile phone out to make a call. This is a good format for those using the busy street method which we will cover later on. Hand signals should be an awkward combination of obvious but subtle. Obvious to the other team members what it is that is being communicated but subtle enough not to stand out to other members of the general public. Operatives should avoid using known military hand signals.

Mobile Phones and Chat Apps – As time has passed, mobile phones are becoming the preferred method to communicate. Whatsapp groups can be created in seconds which can be utilised to pass information, images and video footage. Skype groups can be created and used to create an open line for a number of operatives. In other words, this allows anyone with a good data connection to communicate live with anyone else who is a participant of that group. The downside to this, however, is that it drains the phone battery relatively quickly as well as eating up the phone's data.

RELEVANT LEGISLATION

Being a surveillance operative is a very ‘legally sensitive’ occupation. That is, you can easily find yourself on the wrong side of the law if precautions are not taken or if you are simply unaware of the relevant legislation. In most countries you will require a licence to mount covert observations upon an individual or to conduct any other form of private investigation. I strongly recommend that you seek legal advice prior to undertaking any such task in a country in which you are unfamiliar with the laws or regulations. In the UK, our Security Industry Authority (SIA) are coming ever closer to releasing the new Private Investigator licence which will enable individuals to conduct both surveillance and investigations.

We are now going to discuss the relevant legislation that impacts us as surveillance operatives whilst in the UK. What you will probably find is that there are some very similar items of legislation in different countries as there are in the UK.
We will look at the following:

- Health and Safety at Work Act 1974.
- Human Rights Act 1998.
- Protection from Harassment Act 1997.
- Regulations of Investigatory Powers Act 2000.
- Legislation that impacts photography and videography.
- Vehicle tracking.
- Telephony.

You are probably looking at this thinking, how on earth does the Human Rights Act 1998 or the Protection from Harassment Act 1997 come into play as a surveillance operative? Why do I need to know this? Interestingly, knowing this item of legislation enables you to understand how RIPA impacts those affected by it.

I am of the opinion that anyone that works in a professional field should know the laws that affect them and their work. Having said that, you are not expected to remember every act word by word but you should know what's lawful and what's unlawful. Let us now go over them one by one.

The Health and Safety at Work Act 1974

There are two main sections that impact us in this act, Section 2 and Section 7. Section 2 places legal responsibility on employers to ensure 'so far as reasonably practicable the health and safety and welfare at work of all of his employees' (*Health and Safety at Work Act 1974 a*). What is outlined in this section is that the onus is placed upon employers to ensure that their employees or contractors or whatever it is are safe whilst at work. However, that section of the act does not completely remove an operative (employee or contractor) from the equation. I will explain this in a moment but just to give you some further insight, employers under the legislation must provide the following:

• **Policy statements** - A policy statement, in essence, is a document that outlines what policies the business has in place.

• **Risk assessments** - A risk assessment is something that is conducted by the company or an employee of the company to ensure that all potential risks to the employee or to anyone who is impacted by the employee's omissions have been identified and taken into consideration along with how to counteract them. So if for example, you are working in an environment which is relatively clean, take a hotel room for example, then there are not going to be many hazards. But there may be trip hazards. So if the person who occupies the hotel room has not taken the time to clean the room then there may be trip hazards. Therefore, this will go in the risk assessment and another element of risk assessment will ask what actions have been taken to reduce the risk of that impacting the employee. In more hazardous environments such as building sites, the risk assessments are far more detailed.

• **Procedures detailing what to do in conflict situations** - There is more content that goes into procedures detailing what to do in conflict situations. As a technical surveillance countermeasure operative you're very unlikely to come into conflict or any situation whereby you would need to manage conflict, but based on this element of the act, there are supposed to be procedures detailing what to do should a situation arise.

• **Procedures to check and review safety precautions** - This would be inclusive of procedures to ensure that all practices are relevant, up to date and regularly reviewed.

• **Appropriate training and a safe environment** - How do we ensure that we are sending our operative to a safe location? There will probably be a checklist. We need to go through that checklist to ensure that there are safety precautions in place. Anyone that fulfills a professional role needs to, of course, have the appropriate training and technical surveillance countermeasure operatives are no different.

• **A safe working environment** - We are expected to provide a safe environment as far as reasonably practicable for an operative.

• **Safe work and practices** - This will be a document that outlines what it is that you need to do to operate within the boundaries of what are considered safe.

• **Support for concerns about abuse and aggression** - Support for concerns about abuse or aggression. This will probably be a document that outlines what needs to happen should there be a concern about abuse or aggression within the workplace or as a result of the employees work.

• **Support following violent incidents** - Again, this will be a policy that outlines what needs to be done if there is a violent incident. A checklist going through exactly what needs to happen should something of this nature occur.

Section 7 of the Act relates directly to the employees, the contractors or the operatives where it states that they must take reasonable care for the health and safety of himself and of other persons who may be affected by his acts or emissions at work. This places the onus not only on the employer who is the person that is potentially deploying the operative on an operation, but also the operative themselves. In other words, the employer does have a duty of care to ensure that the extensive list outlined above has been fulfilled, but there is also responsibility of the operative who needs to take into consideration their own health and safety as well as that of others who may be affected. What this outlines is it removes the possibility of you being able to make any claim under this Act if you have done something that contravenes your own health and safety. Why is it relevant? Because as a surveillance operative, you are obviously going to be expected to carry out covert observations, some of which may involve a level of risk. Under Section 7 of the Health and Safety Work Act 1974, you as an operative are responsible for your own health and safety. Risk assessments should be carried out continuously and dynamically to ensure that you maintain the highest level of personal security.

The Human Rights Act 1998

The Human Rights Act 1998 the Human Rights Act, or HRA for short, is a parliamentary Act which was passed through parliament as a result of the European Convention on Human Rights (ECHR). We will not take the time to look through the entire act, only the relevant Article 8 which outlines the right to respect for private and family life. It states;

Section 1
'Everyone has the right to respect for his private and family life, his home and his correspondence.' (The Human Rights Act 1998 (HRA 1998) Art 8 a)

Section 2
'There shall be no interference by public authority with the exercise of this right except such as in accordance with the law and is necessary in a democratic society in the interests of national security, public safety or the economic well-being of the country for the prevention of disorder or crime for the protection of health or morals or for the protection of the rights and freedoms of others.' (HRA 1998 Art 8 b)

What I normally do during the training courses that we hold in the UK and abroad is ask people to look at those sections and identify what allows people, in theory, to essentially spy on one another. When you look at it closely it is the element that outlines the fact that there should be no interference by "*public authorities*".

Obviously, individuals are not public authorities. As we mentioned earlier on, and the other reason that I highlight this is because it actually leads us onto another relatively important aspect of the law that impacts surveillance operatives. This is the Regulation of Investigatory Powers Act 2000 or 'RIPA' for short. What this outlines is when and how a public authority is able to breach sections 1 and 2 of HRA. If you look at section 2 again, I will highlight exactly what I mean. It states, "*There shall be no interference by public authority with the exercise of this right except such as in accordance with the law and is necessary in a democratic society in the interests of national security*". (HRA 1998 Art 8 c)

Now, think about which public authorities play a role in maintaining national security. We can assume that it is Mi5.
It also states "*public safety*", that is questionably the police.
"*The economic well-being of the country*". Mi5 once again, possibly others.
"*for the prevention of disorder or crime*". The police.
"*for the protection of health or morals*". Possibly Mi5 and the police. The list goes on but I think you understand the point that I am trying to make.

What RIPA does is allow article 8 or HRA to be breached however, it has to be one of those reasons that I have just outlined and that are outlined in the bill because there needs to be the ability for public authorities to bypass them as they will need to investigate crime, as well as protecting democratic interests. The same applies for a public authority to be able to investigate you in a way that contravenes this. They have to acquire something that they refer to literally as a "RIPA" and it depends on what public authority it is as to the process of them acquiring that power.

As an example, if it is a police officer or CID officer investigating an individual, they would need to acquire a report if they wanted to mount covert observations upon them. In constabularies across the UK, a RIPA can only be granted by someone who holds a Superintendent rank or higher. They investigating officer(s) will have to present the reasons why they believe that a RIPA should be granted.

The Human Rights Act 2000 goes on to say that it "*only binds public bodies and not individuals*" (HRA 1998 Art 8 d). This clarifies that fact that it is not individuals who are prohibited under this act. It continues to say "*so there is still no general right to protection from invasion of privacy by other individuals and society. This means that you cannot sue your neighbour, or a private company, for invading your privacy. However, because the courts are public authorities, and so have a duty to act compatibly with the Convention rights, and because of the obligation on courts to interpret statutory law compatibly with Convention rights wherever possible, if you have some other ground to bring a claim to court, then once you are before the court you can ask the court to protect your Article 8 rights, and the court will have a duty to do so if possible.*" (HRA 1998 Art 8 d). In essence what that is saying is, the Human Rights Act does not actually bind or does not affect or prevent private individuals or private companies from invading your privacy but there are other pieces of legislation that do. So if you are going to bring a claim against an individual or a company for invading your privacy by breach of your article 8 rights under the Human Rights Act, then you have to have some other legal reason for that.

Protection from Harassment Act 1997

1 Prohibition of harassment.

(1)A person must not pursue a course of conduct

(a)which amounts to harassment of another, and

(b)which he knows or ought to know amounts to harassment of the other.

(2)For the purposes of this section, the person whose course of conduct is in question ought to know that it amounts to harassment of another if a reasonable person is in possession of the same information would think the course of conduct amounted to harassment of the other.

(3)Subsection

(1) does not apply to a course of conduct if the person who pursued it shows

(a)that it was pursued for the purpose of preventing or detecting crime,

(b)that it was pursued under any enactment or rule of law or to comply with any condition or requirement imposed by any person under any enactment, or

(c)that in the particular circumstances the pursuit of the course of conduct was reasonable.

2 Offence of harassment.
(1)A person who pursues a course of conduct in breach of section 1 is guilty of an offence.
(2)A person guilty of an offence under this section is liable on summary conviction to imprisonment for a term not exceeding six months, or a fine not exceeding level 5 on the standard scale, or both.

The level five element is not a monetary figure because as time goes on, the economy grows, inflation rises and therefore the amounts over time will increase. If you were sentenced one hundred years ago the judge may have found it necessary to fine the defendant somewhere in the region of five pounds whereas now, this would probably be laughed at. So, level five will vary as time goes on.

Photography and Videography

Photography and videography is quite an interesting area because there are several different items of legislation that impact it. I have therefore attempted to summarise it in one sentence followed by a lengthy explanation.
You are able to take photographs or video footage of anyone or anything as long as you are in a public place.

Whether you are doing this covertly or overtly, you must ensure that where you are shooting (photography terms) from is a public place. This applies whether you are taking imagery or footage of an individual or property unless it is protected, for some reason, by the Official Secrets Act. If you are standing outside a school and are standing on the public highway as weird as it sounds (and I don't encourage you to do it for obvious reasons) but technically you can take photographs of the children in the playground. I use this as an extreme example and once again, I do not condone it or encourage you to test this in any way. As long as you are on the public highway, no one can really tell you to stop unless a police constable asks you to move on. Do not confuse the 'public place' element with a building that is open to the public because most buildings are owned by someone. Museums and libraries are good examples of this. Most are Crown property so you can be asked to leave or stop what you are doing or be searched upon arrival which would limit someone's ability to take covert photography in the first place. This content is part of the covert surveillance training programme that I wrote many years ago and it is to clarify that you are able to take that videography or photo photography as you are on the public highway.

Vehicle Tracking Devices

Vehicle tracking is a very interesting and debated part of the law but we need to pay attention to one of the courses I wrote involving the deployment of vehicle trackers as it is a covert surveillance course and the investigation company does actually deploy vehicle trackers for investigative purpose and security purposes. We do actually demonstrate how to deploy VTDs when people attend the surveillance training programme in person whether that be in the UK or overseas.

Candidates practice placing the devices on after a theoretical lesson on how to do so. The reason for this is so that they can understand where they should look for the devices. But there is much debate about what is lawful and what is unlawful because as it appears on the face of it, it should be unlawful. Technically it is not because, as a private company or a private individual we are not bound by Article 8 of the Human Rights Act 1998. However, if that vehicle is on private property it may amount to trespass. Interestingly, trespass as many people view it is not actually a crime in itself.

As far as the law is concerned in England and Wales, you only are trespassing if you are on someone's land with the intention to do something else. In other words, it is usually what the person has gone there with the intention to do that amounts to an offence for which they may be prosecuted. As an extreme example, if I entered someone's land with the intention to cause harm to an individual, I would be arrested not for trespass but for the intention to cause that individual harm and that conviction would vary depending on what actually happened. It has been argued before that deploying a vehicle tracking device onto someone's vehicle is trespassing and therefore unlawful. Technically not the case. The question of invasion of privacy has also been raised but, as you have just read, under article 8 of HRA, you as an individual are not bound.

So is vehicle tracking strictly lawful? My advice has always been that it is lawful if it is justified.

I want you to be aware of what laws may impact vehicle tracking is because you may be asked by a client, so it is therefore important for you to understand that it is not technically illegal in this country because there are no laws that I am aware of that directly prevent you from doing it. However, if you enter someone's land you have to break a fence to gain access then, that may amount to breaking and entering which is illegal. If the target vehicle is inside and you know that you are probably going to have to break and enter the property to deploy the device then that again is obviously illegal but as far as just putting a tracker on a vehicle, there is no law that prevents someone from doing so.

Telephony

Telephony is relatively straightforward. You cannot record a telephone call without both parties being aware and consenting. Let me clarify, when you call a bank or financial institution (who are legally obliged for regulation purposes to record their telephone calls), you will hear a message that says something to the effect of "your call may be recorded for training and quality purposes". That is the point at which it is disclosed to you that the telephone call is being recorded and your consent is given by you remaining on the line. If you record a telephone call without consent and attempt to use it as evidence in court it will not be admissible.

SUMMARY

We have the Health and Safety at Work Act 1974 which is relevant because you are responsible for your own safety and that comes into play when you deploy to a location to conduct an op. If you feel that you are not safe or you are in a hazardous environment or your safety may be at risk for some other reason then you should not continue as you are, under Section 7, responsible for your own health and safety. The Human Rights Act 1998 is relevant because it outlines the fact that individuals are not protected from invasion of privacy by other individuals unless some other piece of legislation prevents them from doing so. The Protection From Harassment Act 1997 outlines what actually constitutes harassment. If someone asks you to stop following them, you have to stop. Why is that relevant? Well if you suffer the misfortune of being compromised, the subject may ask you to stop following them. They are telling them you to stop, it is verbally stated and so if you continue to do so, it will amount to an offense of harassment. Is it illegal to record in someone's telephone conversations without the consent of all parties involved in the conversation.

Having good and up to date legal knowledge will set you apart in your area of expertise in comparison with other operatives or service providers.

INTERNATIONAL LAW

Legislature

noun

1. The legislative body of a country or state.

International Law, more formally referred to as ‘public law’, is generally considered as law that is created by countries in an effort to oversee how they deal with one another, with a specific aim of promoting goodwill, whilst not neglecting their own interests or those of their citizens. In this context, however, this chapter will explore generic areas of legislation that may be applicable to operatives and companies in all countries and states. In essence, it seeks to shed light on what legal implications are likely to be relevant to those planning to operate in a country other than the UK. Something that should be considered is that some nations have local, district or state legislatures. In essence, this means that some laws will vary from region to region or state to state. The United States is a good example of this, as they have state laws and federal laws that can both impact the security industry simultaneously, but in different ways. The sections to follow are not collectively exhaustive and as such, legal advice should be sought prior to providing any services involving the use of covert surveillance.

Health & Safety Laws

This is an important aspect and impacts not only anyone who conducts a surveillance operation, but also those who may be affected by another's omissions. In other words, the operative's health and safety is one thing and should be of the utmost importance but so should anyone else who may be impacted by their work.

Insurances

Having the correct insurance is extremely important. It protects the operative, business, business owner, the clients and the general public. In some countries this may not be a legal requirement per se however, it will provide the necessary cover to legally protect those affected.

Licensing Requirements

With respect to the provision of investigation services, many countries require operatives (and sometimes businesses) to be licenced. This is usually to ensure that industry standards are met and maintained. It is more common, however, for this to be the case for services such as personal security rather than private investigators. Nonetheless, it is advisable that research is conducted in order to establish exactly what the local requirements are with respect to licensing.

Reporting & Evidencing Requirements

This element is very difficult to summarise primarily because of the two main legal systems that exist in most countries. They are the common law legal system and the civil law legal system. Confusingly, the civil law legal system does not relate to civil law as we recognise it in terms of the disparity of criminal law and civil law for example. It is not within the scope of this book to define the difference between the two systems however, it is worth considering that the fact that there are two, very different systems and as such the way in which evidence may be presented in court will vary considerably. This could have an impact on the way in which it is collected because of evidential procedures that are likely to be in place as a result of the guidance or regulations set out by the courts or legislature.

Having said that, there are generic components with regards to report writing or evidencing in general that will be required, regardless of legal system, nation or any other such impacting factors. Each element is discussed in other chapters. These are as follows:

- The recording of date and timings.
- Location of evidence acquired.
- Photographing evidence.
- Truthful statements.
- Forensics.

Data Protection

Protecting the data belonging to a client is of the utmost importance. Typically, this is the responsibility of the service provider as opposed to the individual operative although, there will be times when the operative is responsible for client data even if it is their name and address.

Laws relating to data protection will vary from country to country and in some, may not even exist. Others will have very stringent regulations about how personal or protected data is handled. Regardless of this, as those who are operating within the security sector, client data should not only be respected, it should be kept as secure as possible.

OPERATIONAL BRIEFINGS

An operational briefing is a collection of information received by the operative which is designed to provide as much relevant and useful intelligence to assist them to better carry out their task. There is often a level of ambiguity relating to exactly what information can be given to a surveillance operative as a result of a common fear of breaching data protection regulations. This is a misinterpretation or simply a complete misunderstanding of data protection legislation. The new General Data Protection Regulations (GDPR) which is a directive set out by the EU, allows data to be transferred between companies and it's agents. This includes employees and subcontractors. It is relevant because in order for an operative to be expected to be able to carry out their task successfully, they should be given as much intelligence as reasonably practicable.

The method in which an operational briefing will be delivered to the individual carrying the operation out will vary. However, the basic components should remain the same. Every company I have ever worked for has either given the briefing verbally or by email.

Please see the basic elements that an op briefing may comprise of:

Start Date – Of the commencement of the operation.

Start Location – where the operation will start from.

Timings – Start and finish time of the op. On occasions, there may be a start time but no finish time. This is owing to the common unpredictability of the subject's movements but may be governed by the client's budget. A briefing may appear as 0900hrs – TBC (To Be Continued).

Intelligence – Any information that will have an affect the operation and/ or support the operative.

Sit Rep – Information detailing the overall situation which explains why the operation has been authorised. This is something that most companies do not provide the operative with. In my personal opinion, it is a vital piece of information that can on occasion assist the operative in completing a successful operation.

Mode of Transportation - It is vital that we know how the subject will travel around. In fact, HQ should ask the client how the subject intends to travel because it will affect which operative is equipped to carry out the operation. It may also determine how many operatives are deployed.

Primary Objectives – The main goal(s) that the client hopes the operation will achieve.

Secondary Objectives – The less important goals. Some that the client would like but are not vital.

SOE Mobile Number - Having the subject's mobile telephone number is not always possible and is sometimes frowned upon however, it can be useful to the operative to help them identify or confirm the subject's identity should they find themselves in a position where they are unsure.

SOE - So what do we need to know about the SOE before deploying on a surveillance operation?

A – Age
B – Build
C – Clothing
D – Distinguishing Features
E – Elevation
F – Face
G – Gait
H – Hair

Age – the age of the subject.

Build – This is how the client would describe the physical frame of the subject. For example, slim, well built, obese.

Clothing – On many occasions the subject's attire will be impossible to predict. Unless for example, if the client lives or works with the subject. The A-H method is given from the feet upwards starting from describing the footwear, then the trousers and working your way up vertically. The reason for this is so that if the subject is smart enough to change his/ her appearance, they are more likely to change their top half because of time restraints whilst being followed. Therefore footwear and leg-wear are at the top of the list for quick referral.

Distinguishing Features – This can include scars, tattoos, birth marks etc. All of which can assist the operative to identify the subject.

Elevation – The height of the subject can be measured however you prefer but will probably be given in feet and inches as opposed to a metric form of measurement.

Face – This seems to confuse most people as they tend to get it confused with Distinguishing Features. This part of the description relates to the shape of the face. Although this may seem odd, it is what it means. Maybe they just couldn't find another word for F?

Gait – This refers to the stance of a person. How they stand and how they walk. For most people this would be average but there are some cases where someone may have a slight limp for example.

Hair – As it says, this section would be used not only to describe the colour, length etc but also any facial hair.

IC Codes

What isn't included in an A-H description is the race of a subject. The Police in the UK use the following to describe the apparent ethnicity of an individual:

IC1 – White person

IC2 – Mediterranean person

IC3 – African/Caribbean person

IC4 – Pakistani, Indian, Nepalese, Maldivian, Sri Lankan, Bangladeshi, or any other (South) Asian person

IC5 – Chinese, Japanese, Korean or South-East Asian person

IC6 – Arabic, Egyptian, Tunisian, Algerian or Maghreb person

IC7 - Origin unknown

RECONNAISSANCE

"Time spent in reconnaissance is seldom time wasted". (Arthur Wellesley (Duke of Wellington), Victor of Waterloo)

Covert reconnaissance comes in two forms; physical and digital. Unfortunately, in the private sector, companies are restricted by a client's budget. As such, a surveillance operation seldom has paid time for a recce op factored in. For this reason, an operative may consider conducting either a digital recce or a very brief recce shortly prior to the operation start time. My personal preference is the latter as it is more relevant and will take other additional factors such as foot traffic, weather, lighting and visibility into consideration which cannot be ascertained during a digital recce.

As you may have already guessed, a digital recce is one where an operative utilises open source tools such as digital maps and street view to identify some of the main components in an effort to support the planning and preparation of a surveillance task.

Planning a Recce

All recces for surveillance operations should obviously be conducted covertly. Doing this will also increase your experience in covert ops. Some recces can be done overtly

when we are on protection duty for a celebrity and the venue knows that he or she is due for arrival for example, but that is a completely different topic.
Reconnaissance is only really effective if it is conducted at the same time and the same day as the operation due commencement. Why? Several reasons;

Traffic – Traffic will vary depending on the time of day and the day of the week. Rush hour and the school runs should be taken into consideration. This will only really affect you if you are on a mobile surveillance operation (in a vehicle).

Human Traffic – If your operation is going to be in a city centre, obviously human traffic is going to impact your visibility or ability to blend in.

Other Scheduled Occurrences – There could be absolutely anything that may have an effect on your operation. One example could be, a recycling van passing through a residential street where your subject lives. It could literally be anything. I hope this highlights my point on why the recce should be done on the same day and time as the due commencement of the operation.

Objectives of a Recce Operation

Exit Route – It is extremely important that operatives ensure that they have a safe and quick getaway strategy. If on a mobile operation, they are much safer sitting in the driver's seat with the key in the ignition and the doors locked.

Determine Potential Hazards – This includes pretty much anything that can either breach your own personal safety or lead to a compromise. This can include things such as, the possibility of being blocked in because it is a dead end street, or parking directly outside a neighbour's house who may inform the subject or police of your presence. Having the police come to greet you on an op will only draw unwanted attention.

Determine Entrances & Exits – This is more inclined towards buildings. If the start point is in a restaurant for example, it is important to know if there is more than one entrance. It is no good for an operative to watch one door waiting for the subject to come in when there is an entrance at the back or around the corner.

Determine Best Positions for Operatives – If you are a team leader, it is up to you to position your team members. Entrances and exits should be taken into consideration in addition to the use of hard and soft cover.

Hard and Soft Cover

Hard cover can be defined as a position whereby it is a physical impossibility for the subject to see an operative whereas soft cover is a position where the subject is able to see them but they are blending in with the everyday movements of the other members of the public.

Examples of hard cover:

- Inside a building
- Inside a surveillance vehicle
- Behind a large vehicle
- Behind a wall or other solid, opaque structure

Examples of soft cover:

- Bus stop
- Using the reflection of a shop window
- Blending in with a crowd

PERSONAL SECURITY

The Importance of Personal Security

As a surveillance operative, personal security is of the utmost importance. There are two aspects of security that surveillance operatives should be conscious of;

1. The security that will help negate the possibility of our immediate safety being compromised.
2. Privacy - The protection of anything that could compromise personal intel which could affect our personal/ family life.

With respect to the first point, there are a number of factors that will assist you to achieve this whether or not you are trained in some form of security. Namely, maintaining a constant level of awareness by employing dynamic risk assessment models and understanding how to control your adrenaline.

Dynamic Risk Assessments

Dynamic assessments is by far the most common type of assessment you will ever conduct. You do it every day probably without realising it. When you cross the road, you look left and right to assess whether it is safe or not for you to cross. This is you "dynamically" assessing. Dynamic essentially means 'live', 'current' and 'ongoing'.

There are three main acronyms we can utilise to when conducting a dynamic risk assessment:

TACT

T - Think (Safety First)
A - Assess (The Situation)
C - Consider (Your Options)
T - Take (Action)

POP

P - People
O - Objects (such as weapons)
P - Places

POP is also used in another format, SEW:

SEW

S - Subjects (people)
E - Environment (place)
W - Weapons (objects)

CONTROLLING ADRENALINE

Preparing The Body & Mind For an Incident

Being unaware, ignorant or generally switched off to your surroundings can have a seriously negative affect to your reactions as you will inevitably be taken by surprise should an incident occur. Having poor reactions can and will lead to a disaster. Best case scenario, it will make you look unprepared, unaware and therefore unprofessional. As a surveillance operative mounting observations from a vehicle, an adrenaline dump can have a profound, negative effect on basic motor skills preventing them from being able to put the keys in the ignition.

Adrenaline

Adrenaline is a hormone that is released by glands that are located near the kidneys. Our bodies react to adrenaline by increasing our heart rate and therefore apply more oxygen to muscles that require it such as the muscles groups in our legs. Because of the unfair distribution of oxygen, a dump of adrenaline can quite often cause us to suffer from what is commonly known as "brain freeze". This can lead to a loss of control of a reasonable thought process and our basic motor skills.

You may have heard of the phrase "Fight or Flight". Well, a dump of this hormone can put us into a phase of "Fight", "Flight" or "Freeze".

Fight

A quick fright can cause someone to lash out. There are hundreds of YouTube videos showing these reactions of "Pranks Gone Wrong". Whilst it can sometimes be funny to watch this kind of footage, it is also very interesting to observe the human self defense system kick in and react in this manner. As a bodyguard, this could be seen as a positive or negative reaction. My opinion though, is that all reactions should be calculated whenever possible. Yes surprises can happen, but it is the job of a surveillance operative to anticipate them and react accordingly.

Flight

Possibly the most common reaction to a fright is to run. If you decide to do this then make sure you take your equipment and any compromising material with you.

Freeze

Adrenaline can have a seriously negative effect if an incident occurs whilst you're not prepared. This is known as "Freeze". An adrenaline overload will simply cause our bodies to stop without knowing what to do next. As you can imagine, this is the worst scenario for a surveillance operative whilst at work.

Controlling Adrenaline

We cannot control whether or not we have a dump of adrenaline or indeed our body's reaction to it, but to avoid suffering from brain freeze or any other negative reaction that can occur shortly afterwards, you should apply a “drip feed” of anticipation. Thinking about an incident occurring can help better prepare our bodies to react positively to the adrenaline that is inevitable. Also, constantly monitoring the situation in your immediate surroundings can help negate this.

To apply the “drip feed”, simply think of potential incidents that can occur. Think as realistically as possible and think about your reactions. What are you going to do? How are you going to do it? What are your priorities?

COOPER'S COLOUR CODES

Created by Jeff Cooper, a retired US Marine, Cooper’s colour codes provide a simple way to promote situational awareness.

Code White

Code white is unaware, switched off and ignorant to your surroundings. You could relate this mindset to the “Unaware Subject” discussed during the surveillance section of this book because it makes up a vast majority of the general public.

Code White is a dangerous place for the surveillance operative to be. Should you fall victim to some form of attack whilst in this mind set, you would be taken completely by surprise and probably be incapable of protecting yourself adequately.

Code Yellow

Code yellow is an ideal mindset for the surveillance operative, subject to the threat level. In fact, I would encourage most people, including members of the general public, to try and be in code yellow as much as possible. Think of it as a mindset whereby you are running possible scenarios through your thoughts along with your consequential reactions. What are you going to do if the subject gets into a vehicle whilst you are on foot? What will your actions on drills be should someone attempt to open the car doors whilst you are inside?

Code yellow will help you better prepare for incidents should they occur. It will be the “drip feed” mentioned earlier. You will more than likely find yourself drifting from code yellow to code white from time to time but it is your responsibility to ensure that you remain in code yellow as much as possible to prevent being caught unaware. After a while, you will probably notice yourself living in this mindset indefinitely.

Code Orange

This is where you have reason to become concerned about something specific. Your awareness in code yellow has now forced you into being aware of something specific. Your mindset has shifted from general awareness to now assessing the one specific thing that has put it there. You are now seriously considering possible actions on, escape routes etc.

You will begin to feel adrenaline which should not have a

negative effect on your abilities thanks to the "drip feed" process. You will probably maintain this heightened level of awareness several hours after noticing a potential threat posed to yourself or your team.

Code Red

Whilst in code yellow your positive level of awareness spotted something unusual or concerning that put you into code orange. You then started to think about possible actions on drills, possible escape routes etc. Now you have to implement those actions! Whatever you thought was going to happen, has now happened. Code red will see you have a further adrenaline dump which, if not managed properly, will prevent you from reacting positively.

PRIVACY

Privacy is also a very important aspect to consider in relation to maintaining your personal security. The most obvious example of this is the vehicle in which you decide to use for operational purposes. The registered details of this vehicle should never pertain to your home address. Instead, it is advisable that you seek to engage the services of a virtual office. This will be the registered address that is visible to anyone who seeks to establish who and where the vehicle pertains to. There are a few downsides to this however. These include; the additional ongoing expense of a virtual office, ensuring that you check mail there regularly and having to pay business insurance as it is now officially used for ‘business’ purposes. These do not, in my opinion, outweigh the downside of a hostile subject (and potentially their associates) turning up at your front door whilst your family are inside eating dinner.

A less obvious example may be a parking permit which is permanently on display in the windscreen and therefore easily overlooked or forgotten. Permits often denote the general area or in some cases, the exact street in which the owner resides. Take care to ensure that there is nothing on display in your operational vehicle that denotes something personal about you or where you live.

SUMMARY

The personal safety of an operative is of the utmost importance. Utilising very informed yet basic strategies such as Cooper’s colour codes whilst understanding how adrenaline will have a negative impact if not properly managed, ensures a good level of consciousness relating to danger and therefore, safety. The conduction of continuous dynamic assessments will assist the operative achieve this.

ACTIONS ON DRILLS

One of the main reasons that recce ops are conducted is so that we can ascertain the relevant information about a property/ venue that will better equip the team to put in contingencies and establish the best possible actions on drills that will ensure a positive outcome of the surveillance task. The information that comes as a result of a recce is the layout of the building, entrances/ exits etc. With this information, an operative or team leader can determine a number of facts that will not only affect the actions on drills (AODs), but also help to decide upon contingencies if required. Actions on drills are often confused with standard operating procedures but it is important to be able to distinguish between the two. It is, therefore, that we will compare both (AODs and SOPs) in this chapter. Contingencies (or contingency plans) will also be considered for additional contrast.

What is The Difference?

Actions on Drills

Actions on Drills are pre-arranged actions that team members should take should an incident occur. These incidents should be anticipated in order for the AODs to be relevant and appropriate. A good example of this could be if the subject enters a building that is already known to be associated with them but has a complex layout. This fictitious example shown in figure 45 Could be applicable for op Luma or India Charlie.

Figure 45

The actions on drills for this example could be as follows:

- At least one operative takes a photograph of the building for reporting purposes.
- One operative follows the subject into the building and acquires covert imagery.
- Other operatives implement a trigger system for when the subject leaves.
- The trigger should endeavour to acquire an image of the subject departing the building.

Actions on drills can only be put into place once a recce has been conducted because every situation is different meaning that all factors need to be carefully considered. They will not be necessary for every op. AODs can either be chosen by the TL, 2IC or together as a team. But it is imperative that all team members are aware of their individual responsibilities.

SOPs

SOPs can be described as a set of rules that are set out by an organisation in order to ensure that the operatives are conducting their roles effectively. They are often in the form of a checklist and should be adhered to by anyone who has had them delegated to them so that no step is overlooked.

To make them as effective as possible, some companies issue SOPs before, during and after a task has been completed.

If something was to occur during a surveillance operation, the steps taken would not necessarily be standard operating procedures. This is a common misconception. Actions on Drills are a series of pre-arranged steps that are taken for a preconceived occurrence. AODs are discussed in more detail in the following chapter. Below are some examples of SOPs that may be given to an operative before, during and after an operation.

Example - Pre-deployment SOPs:

- Confirm receipt of operational briefing.
- Ensure that primary objectives and secondary objectives (if applicable) are fully understood.
- Ensure that all relevant equipment is fully charged and functioning correctly.
- Make sure that cameras have sufficient storage.
- Consider conducting recce op.
- Plan the journey to the start location.

Example - SOPs for when a trigger vehicle is placed into position (with trigger operative concealed inside):

- Once confirmation has been received that the desired parking space/ location is available, park the vehicle ensuring that the trigger has a good line of sight of the anticipated subject departure location.

The steps to follow are for the trigger operative;

- Once parked, conduct a comms check to ensure that you are in range with the rest of the team.
- Take a clear image of the operation start location for report writing purposes.
- Conduct regular comms checks.
- Upon observing the subject, communicate the following with the remainder of the team:
    - That the subject has departed.

- MOT.
- In which direction they are heading.
- Their attire.
- Any other useful information.

The same as AODs, SOPs can either be chosen by the TL, 2IC or together as a team.

Contingencies

Contingency - *Noun* - A provision for a possible event or circumstance.

Basically, this means a Plan B. Should an incident occur, what is the backup plan?

SUMMARY

Actions on drills are a set of pre-established steps that are only put in place for operations that require it and for all operatives concerned. Unlike standard operating procedures, they are not applicable for all tasks and are therefore specific and 'tailor-made'. Conversely, contingencies fall somewhere in the middle with respect to being specific to the operation because they are, more often than not, generic. The use of emergency rendezvous points (ERVs) are commonplace in situations involving hostile subjects. In reality, contingencies are seldom used or considered during surveillance operations in the private sector because of the cost implications that come with the planning and preparation phase. Despite this, it is advisable for substantial plans that could go wrong.

FOOT SURVEILLANCE TECHNIQUES

Contrary to popular belief, foot techniques are there as a guide only and are implemented to mitigate as far as reasonably practicable, the likelihood of being observed by the subject. Remember that surveillance is an art form, not an exact science. Whilst it would be convenient to imagine that there is a set formula on how to deal with each and every scenario, it is simply not the case. The foot methods adopted in conjunction with the effective use of cover are only considered based on the situation at the time in order to reduce the possibility of being seen by the subject thus the likelihood of being completely compromised.

Please note that all drawn images demonstrating foot techniques will denote the subject with an S and positions using the letters A, B and occasionally C. As stated, these are positions that are not to be confused or mischaracterised as operatives. Whilst one operative could be in any of the positions (A, B or C), please be mindful that more than one could adopt it. That said, with regards to the quiet street method there is likely only to be one operative in each position owing to the nature of the situation.

Before moving on, it is important to understand how human memory works and why this is applicable to surveillance.

THE HUMAN BRAIN AND PERIPHERAL AWARENESS

Memory Triggers - *A memory trigger can be described as something that spurs the brain to recollect something transferring it from the unconscious to the conscious memory.*

Understanding how individuals form and access memories may not strike you as the most relevant topic in relation to surveillance however, if you consider the question 'how is a subject likely to become aware of my presence?', your opinion may change slightly.

It is important to firstly point out that a healthy human brain has the ability to store a lot more than many realise. On a busy day in an urban environment, someone may encounter in excess of ten thousand faces and yes, each and every one of those faces are stored in our long term memory.

The human brain consists of about one billion neurons. Each neuron forms about 1,000 connections to other neurons, amounting to more than a trillion connections. If each neuron could only help store a single memory, running out of space would be a problem. You might have only a few gigabytes of storage space, similar to the space in an iPod or a USB flash drive. Yet neurons combine so that each one helps with many memories at a time, exponentially increasing the brain's

memory storage capacity to something closer to around 2.5 petabytes (or a million gigabytes). For comparison, if your brain worked like a digital video recorder in a television, 2.5 petabytes would be enough to hold three million hours of TV shows. You would have to leave the TV running continuously for more than 300 years to use up all that storage. (Douglas Smith, professor of neurosurgery and director of the Center for Brain Injury and Repair at the University of Pennsylvania
(ScientificAmerican, 2020)

The issue comes about when we consider how we access those memories. Without some form of manipulation, the average individual will not be able to recall all of those faces upon demand. That is, of course, unless there is something that 'sticks out' about that face or person. In other words, was there something significant about one particular character that allows someone to recall them from our long term (or subconscious) memory.

In the Hollywood hit movie 'Limitless' the main character Eddie Mora played by Bradley Cooper states "They say we can only access 20 percent of our brains... well, this [drug] lets you access all of it!". There is much discussion about the credibility of this statement however it is widely considered that these figures are probably quite accurate.

A brain does not have two sides in this respect but to assist this explanation, consider that there are two key elements (or sides) to the brain's memory function; *the unconscious memory* and *the conscious memory*. The attributes that 'stick out' can be referred to as 'triggers'. What attributes 'trigger' a memory from the unconscious memory to the conscious memory?

To better assist with this lesson, take a moment to think about the last time that you were in your local high street and try to recollect anyone who you can remember from that timeframe. Really think about this and then consider what it was about that particular person that shifted them from your unconscious to your conscious memory, and be honest. The next page discusses some of the more common 'triggers'.

Attire - Bright, unusual or distinctive clothing will increase the likelihood of someone being triggered into the conscious memory.

Attractiveness - If someone stands out to you because you find them attractive, the chances of remembering them are increased significantly.

Behaviour - Unusual behaviour will stand out and is therefore more likely to be triggered into the conscious memory.

Repeat Sightings - If you see the same person more than two to three times then there is an increased likelihood that you will remember them.

All of the above are should be taken into consideration by the operative when planning a surveillance operation. Doing so will mitigate the likelihood of being triggered into the conscious memory of the subject.

PERIPHERAL AWARENESS

We will now examine how 'memory triggers' impact surveillance operatives based on their correlation with subjects. Firstly, I have broken down the types of subject into three categories based on their levels of awareness. This is an approximation based on hundreds of surveillance tasks.

Each category has its own respective peripheral awareness which are measured by their 'arcs' of vision. The first is an 'unaware' subject who has a peripheral arc of approximately ninety degrees. This is based on a typical individual's arcs when looking straight ahead.

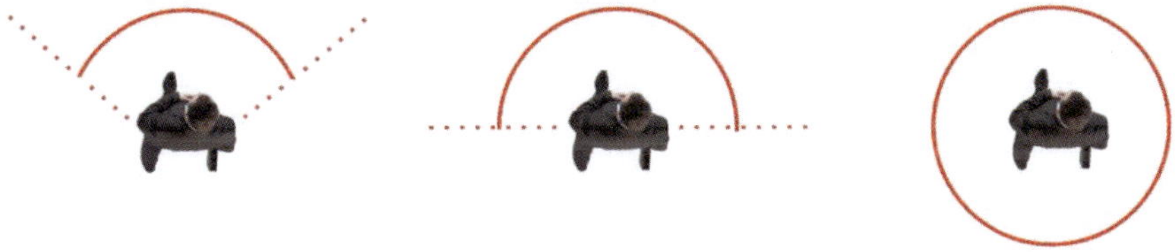

Figure 46 - Arcs of peripheral awareness

UNAWARE

Peripheral Arcs - Up to 90°

Typical Overview - Unaware subjects make up a vast majority of the general public. Average, everyday people going about their business who have no reason to believe that they are being followed.

Compromise Threshold - Roughly speaking, the subject will need to see an operative 3-4 times before they become aware of their presence.

AWARE

Peripheral Arcs - Up to 180°

Typical Overview - Aware subjects are typically those who are slightly more conscious of their surroundings. Maybe someone who considers themselves more likely to be followed, possibly as a result their involvement with petty crime or because they have been followed before.

Compromise Threshold - 2-4 times.

AWARE

Peripheral Arcs - 360°

Typical Overview - This is someone who is either trained in surveillance and counter/ anti-surveillance or someone who is very paranoid about being covertly monitored.

Compromise Threshold - 2 times.

SUMMARY

The operatie must be conscious of the different subject categories. Whilst they are an approximation, they can assist with the planning and preparation phase. It will also help with positioning which is something that is assessed dynamically and is covered in the next chapter. Clothing and appearance must also be taken into careful consideration as this can impact the risk of the subject becoming aware of the operative's presence.

THE QUIET STREET METHOD

Of all the tactical foot drills, the quiet street method is by far the easiest to remember and implement. Before discussing the actual method itself, it is worth mentioning that the answer to the question of what defines a 'busy street' is one that is often received with some degree of ambiguity. A quiet street is not one that is limited by its size but rather by the amount of human and road traffic. In other words, just because a road is wide and in a built-up area does not necessarily mean that it is not one that falls into the category of a quiet street. We could go a step further and say that some streets could be considered quiet on some days and busy on others. Good examples of this can be found in many financial districts that are bustling with vehicles and people during the working week and completely baron on Saturday and Sundays. There is, of course, no real scientific definition of a quiet street in terms of the amount of people and there will almost certainly be times where there is uncertainty when establishing whether or not you are on a quiet or busy street however, it is important to remember that this is simply to help operatives identify the most appropriate method of foot surveillance to be adopted at any given time. The proverbial bridge that helps us overcome the disparity of the two can be overcome with the use of common sense, previous events that have happened during the surveillance period and, in time, experience.

Now that the definition has been somewhat outlined, the operative should seek to establish whether or not they are in/ on a quiet street. As the subject(s) advance on foot, changing directions, stopping and starting, entering and exiting buildings, the operative will naturally assess the situation on an ongoing basis. The level of awareness discussed in the previous chapter should also be taken into consideration with respect to distance. We refer to this as a dynamic assessment. A reoccurring evaluation as to the general environment to help identify what the best foot technique to adopt is.

Now onto the method itself;

Figure 47 - The quiet street method with one operative

Figure 47 Demonstrates the method with one operative being directly behind the subject's position. For the use of more than one operative, as you can see from the very basic example in figure 48, the operative(s) are in 'transit' with one another as well as the subject. This is a phrase that will be repeated a number of times throughout the book and in case you are unaware, in transit simply means to be in-line with the subject. The theory is that the subject's arcs are facing forward and therefore directly behind the subject (being conscious of the distance), is the area where they are least likely to cross over. Even if the subject looked to the right, the arcs still do not cross over as demonstrated in figure 49. This is, at least, the theory. In reality (and in this example) the subject will look for moving vehicles in which case the arcs will encroach on position A. The subject observing an operative does not necessarily mean that they have been compromised. There are many variables that will impact the likelihood of an operative being compromised. These include (but are not limited to); the awareness of the subject, how many times the subject has already observed the operative(s), the layout of the ground, the operatives attire and the operative's reaction once observed by the subject. Once again, this is all theoretical and the operative should be mindful that simply adhering to the relevant techniques does not completely remove the possibility of a compromise, it merely reduces the chances.

This method will almost certainly lead to a temporary loss of visual contact with the subject. To answer how to deal with this very common scenario, please refer to the time/ distance method chapter.

Figure 48 demonstrates the method with one operative being directly behind the subject's position. For the use of more than one operative, as you can see from the very basic example in figure 48, the operative(s) are in 'transit' with one another as well as the subject. This is a phrase that will be repeated a number of times throughout the book and in case you are unaware, in transit simply means to be in-line with the subject. The theory is that the subject's arcs are facing forward and therefore directly behind the subject (being conscious of the distance), is the area where they are least likely to cross over. Even if the subject looked to the right, the arcs still do not cross over as demonstrated in figure 49. This is, at least, the theory. In reality (and in this example) the subject will look for moving vehicles in which case the arcs will encroach on position A. The subject observing an operative does not necessarily mean that they have been compromised. There are many variables that will impact the likelihood of an operative being compromised. These include (but are not limited to); the awareness of the subject, how many times the subject has already observed the operative(s), the layout of the ground, the operatives attire and the operative's reaction once observed by the subject. Once again, this is all theoretical and the operative should be mindful that simply adhering to the relevant techniques does not completely remove the possibility of a compromise, it merely reduces the chances.

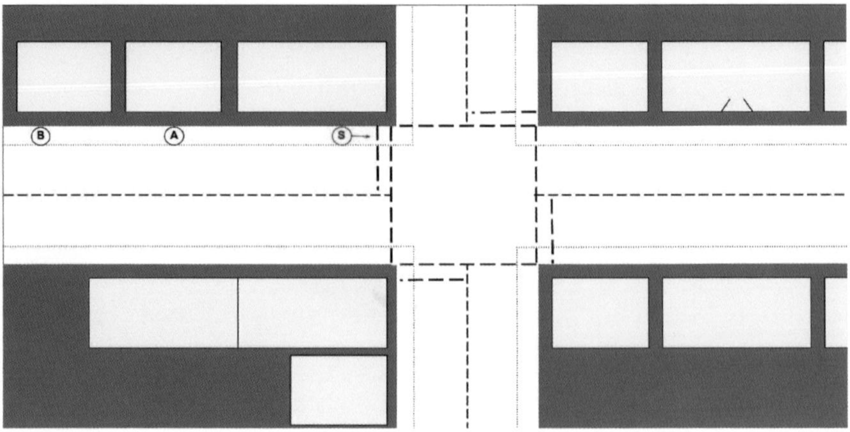

Figure 48 - Two operatives in transit

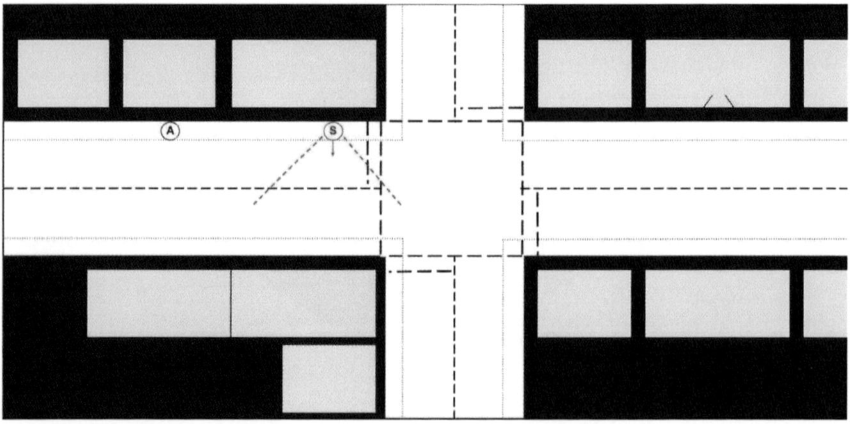

Figure 49 - Subject's arcs when turning to cross the street

SUMMARY

The quiet street method is a commonly used technique that would probably be implemented naturally without having to read this chapter as it is relatively instinctive to follow someone from directly behind when attempting to mount covert observations upon another individual in public. That said, it is good to highlight why it is important in the context of the subject's arcs as this will assist the operative's conscious positioning for this and other methods.

THE BUSY STREET METHOD

The 'ABC' Method

One of the downfalls of having to follow a subject using the quiet street method is that, should they turn a corner the operative(s) may lose sight of them. Unfortunately, given the environment there are not many alternatives without being compromised. A busy street allows a team to utilise a position that enables them to maintain 'eyes on' the subject should they turn a corner, enter a building or make any other such deviation from walking in a straight line.

Much like the quiet street method, this technique relies on the operative or team to be able to establish whether or not the environment constitutes what may be defined as a 'busy street'. Again, the width of the street or road does not, on its own, make the location a busy one. Instead it is the amount of foot and road traffic that does as this directly impacts the operative's ability to maintain observations on the subject. There will be times when a street is clearly a busy one and likewise, examples when a street is considered a quiet one however, the few that fall between the two are defined not by any definitive or scientific formula, but instead by a combination of prior occurrences during the surveillance period, the awareness level of the subject and the gut feeling of the operative based on their experience to mention a few.

This technique is also referred to as 'the ABC method' owing to the three key positions that are implemented in this drill unsurprisingly known as positions A, B and C. The basic image in figure 50 outlines these positions.

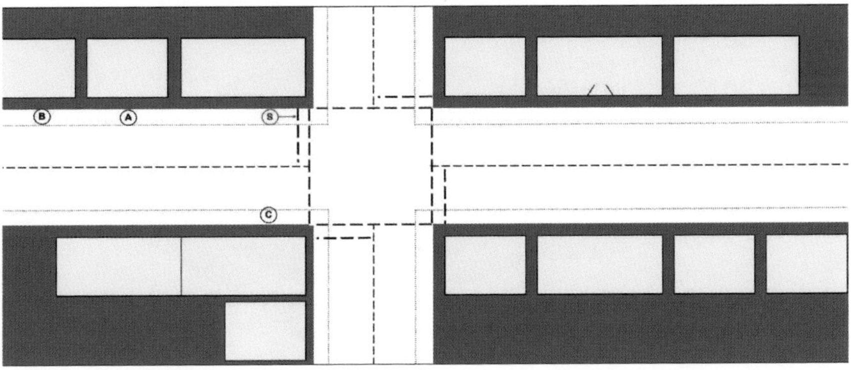

Figure 50 - The ABC Method

Positions A and B remain the same as that in the quiet street method with the only addition being position C. This overcomes the issue discussed at the beginning of this chapter as it is the sole responsibility of the operative(s) in position C to monitor the subject's movements should they deviate from walking in a straight line or in a way that prevents the other two positions from being able to observe them. This is acheived by position C maintaining a perpendicular position with the subject.

The operative or operatives in position C have two key responsibilities; maintaining eyes on the subject as and when they deviate from walking in a straight line and relaying these movements to the remainder of the team prioritising those in position A, as they will be closer to those in position B. The way in which this can be communicated will vary however, it will need to be instantaneous due to the time implications. Because of this, candidates are required to use hand signals during the training courses for which they are given four situations to come up with their own, agreed, subtle hand signals:

1. The subject has stopped.
2. The subject has entered a building.
3. The subject has continued to advance.
4. I have lost the subject.

Alternating Positions

Changing positions is a conversation that often brings some degree of contention. Primarily because of what can be considered to be a global misconception of non-existent rules and formulas within the security industry. Whilst wishing to avoid embarking on a rant, this sector has been poisoned with a myriad of misinformation and incompotent theories that, for some reason, are often widely adopted. In this case, the way in which operatives change positions is regularly challenged during the training courses as some of the candidates who attend have been misinformed or partially trained by an organisation who do not specialise in this field. That said, there are some examples whereby a basic manoeuvre can overcome certain situations. There are two examples of this on the next page.

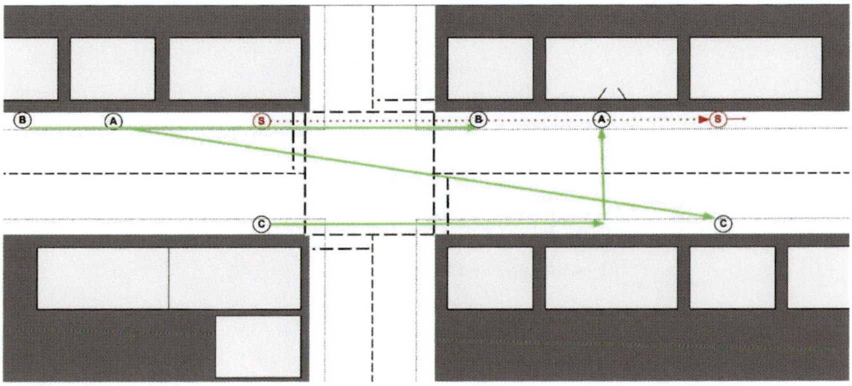

Figure 51

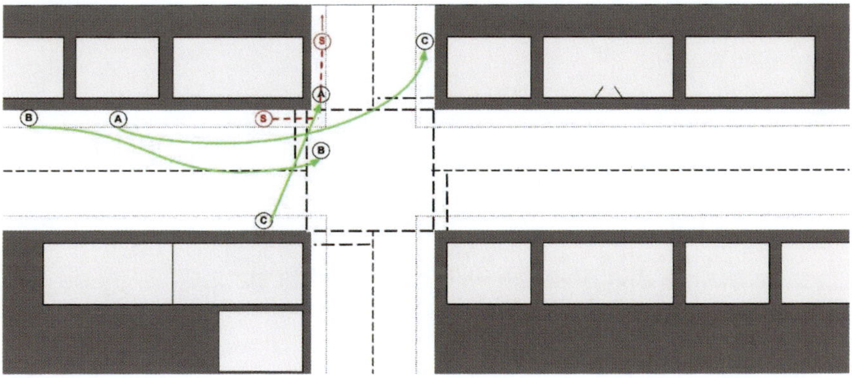

Figure 52

As demonstrated in the images above, there are certain ways in which team members can alternate positions to accommodate the subject's change of direction. However, if all of the possible variables that could occur whilst out on the ground are taken into consideration, there are quite possibly tens of thousands of possibilities in terms of how the team may react. To that end, it is not possible to remember each and every formula for all of these scenarios. So the operative should be mindful that whilst some may say that X, Y and Z should happen if the subject does this or that, the reality is, most situations can be overcome with a combination of good team work and the implementation of common sense.

Common discrepancies with this method

During the surveillance training courses that take place people often challenge this methodology. The most common points are as follows:

1. **"It is easier for the subject to see someone who is practically in line with them."**
Whilst this is true, the reason that the ABC method works is because it is implemented on a busy street. As such, the operative(s) in this position will rely on other people as a use of soft cover thus mitigating that risk.

2. **"What happens if the subject decides to cross the road and turns directly facing position C's location/ area?"**
This is very likely to happen however there are several things to remember here. Firstly, this does not necessarily mean that the subject has been compromised. Actions are taken as an attempt to reduce the chances of the subject's arcs crossing the operative's paths, not completely removing them. Secondly there are at least three operatives to choose from whilst using

this method. This presents an opportunity to switch operatives which of course has its own benefits. Also, the operative may not have even been seen by the subject owing to the use of soft cover (i.e. a crowd).

3. **"What about locations that are not streets or roads?"**
This technique can absolutely be implemented in other busy environments including shopping centres/ malls, public transport terminals etc. The positioning may have to be more malleable however, position C should always be maintained as much as possible.

SUMMARY

The ABC method is a key foot technique that should be adopted by teams of three or more whilst in a busy environment. If there are less than three, the team should endeavour to implement positions A and C because B is somewhat redundant. Utilising pre-arranged hand signals during this period is a good idea owing to the speed at which the subject's movements can be communicated to the rest of the team.

ENTERING A BUILDING

The decision to enter a building should only come as a result of a dynamic assessment of all impacting factors. These include (but are not limited to); the awareness of the subject, how many times the subject has already observed the operative(s), the layout of the ground, the operatives attire and the operative's reaction once observed by the subject. The main factor however, is the size of the building.

This is often a difficult topic for many to grasp. This is primarily owing to industry misconceptions discussed in The Busy Street chapter. Contrary to popular belief, there is no set formula to each scenario. In an attempt to demonstrate this, a number of scenarios will be set out below using the information from op Luma and India Charlie.

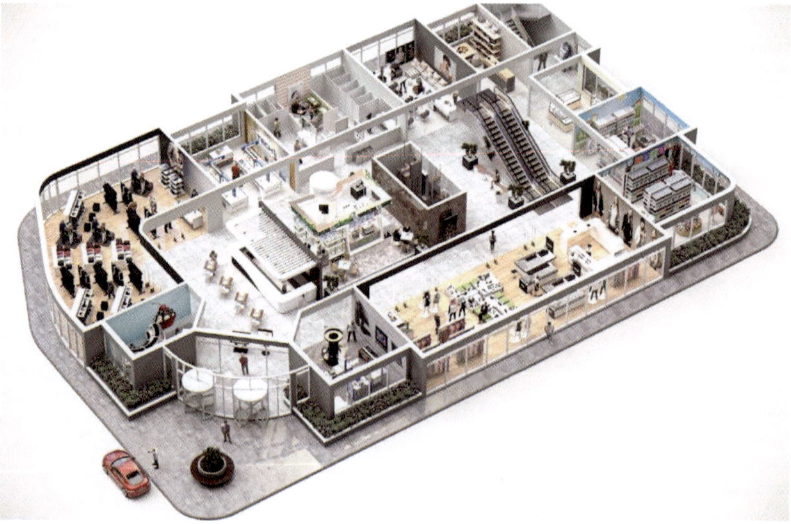

Figure 53 - A shopping centre layout (JerichoDomingo, 2020)

Firstly, take a look at the layout of the ground in figure 53. Consider the circumstances in op Luma and imagine that the subject has entered the shopping centre. Should the operatives enter, remain outside or should only one of them go inside? If your answer is "it depends", then do not feel surprised. But do ask yourself what it depends on? As you think about this, start creating a mental or written list of what your decision would depend upon. Those factors have come about as a result of you not being given the full facts. To demonstrate this, now imagine that the subject from op India Charlie one has entered the same building. What would you do now? If you were one of those who made a decision relatively quickly for the other example then your decision may have now changed. This is because of a change of one impacting factor. If you fell into the category of someone who thought 'it depends' then, you will already have decided that the situation (or sit-rep) is a major contributing factor. Now refer to that list what it was that you thought that it depended upon. It will more than likely consist of some of what has been mentioned in previous chapters including, but not limited to:

- The sit-rep.
- The primary objectives.
- The awareness level of the subject.
- Previous observations.
- Incidents during the current surveillance period.
- Layout of the ground.

• Level/ amount of foot traffic (both inside and outside of the building).
• Level/ amount of road traffic (outside of the building).
• Anticipated next direction/ movements of the subject.

Each of the items above will have their own number of variables. The sit-rep variable has already been demonstrated with op Luma and op India Charlie. Some of these variables will be low in number however, others will be pretty much infinite. The layout of the ground is a good example of this as every location is different thus offering endless variations of this singular factor. This should demonstrate that, contrary to the theory of many, it is not possible to install a set formula for each and every scenario owing to the unlimited amount of possibilities.
That said, if the building is large with the layout unknown to the team then, several steps are advisable:

• One operative follows the subject into the building with three key responsibilities;
• Maintain eyes on the subject's movements and acquire covert imagery.
• Assess (where possible) how many entrances there are.
• Relay this information to the other team members giving them the best opportunity to continue covert observations when the subject leaves the building.

- Other operatives should endeavour to position themselves based on the information provided by the operative who entered. If possible, a trigger system should be implemented.

SUMMARY

Because of the wide range of variables, the theory that there is a set formula as to how an operative or team should respond to a subject entering a building is flawed. If you were one of the instantaneous decision makers to the earlier question '*Should the operatives enter, remain outside or should only one of them go inside?*' then, it could be inferred that, all risk mitigating factors have not been considered and as such the decision is a risk to say the least. However, now that the content of this chapter has been digested, it would be wise to conduct a dynamic assessment in every situation to help ensure that the risk of a compromise is minimised.

PRIME POSITIONING

Prime positioning is an extremely important element of foot surveillance. It enables the operatives to be less visible by mitigating the likelihood of falling within the subject's arcs. More importantly, it can and should be implemented on a dynamic basis when on foot and more specifically when the subject enters a building. To put it plainly, prime positions are those that are employed when a subject enters a building. Whilst in certain circumstances when one or more operatives should enter a building (covered in another chapter), most cases will dictate that prime positions are the more favourable option.

The two main options will depend, greatly, on the layout of the ground along with other factors. The key element to consider is, the foot traffic on the street or the amount of people between the operative(s) and the building in which the subject has entered. This will affect the distance between the operative(s) and the building/ location. The other main consideration is the direction that the subject is likely to head in after departing that location.

In the two images that follow, the subject is currently in the shop with the green and white facade.

Figure 54 - Close prime positioning

Firstly, observe the positions of the operatives in figure 54. They have located themselves relatively close to the entrance of the building in which the subject has entered. This will invariably be because of the amount of people walking in and occupying the ground between them and that entrance. This is the more common form of prime positioning. As the subject departs, their arcs will temporarily be facing forward until they turn left or right. They may also decide to cross the road in which case their arcs will briefly turn as they look for traffic. However, if they do turn left or right their arcs will do the same. This is where many contest that one of those positions will fall into those arcs therefore increasing the risk of a compromise. Whilst this is a valid argument, the operative(s) will already have two key elements to mitigate this risk; distance and foot traffic, both of which will greatly affect the subject's visibility of those positions. The other thing to consider is that, if the team are able to predict which direction the subject is likely to turn then, they will use the opposite flank where the arcs will be facing in the complete opposite direction.

Figure 55 - Wider prime positioning

Figure 55 contains another example with one of the positions being near a shop entrance. This is to highlight one of many things that an operative may do if the subject does depart a building and head in their direction. As shown, they have decided to use the shop window as a form of soft cover, conscious of the fact that there is a good chance that the subject will head towards them after leaving the building that they are currently in. If this does happen, the operative can either continue to stand there and use the window's reflective surface to observe the subjects movements or walk into the same building. The main thing to avoid is quick, sudden movements as this attracts unnecessary attention. Not only of the subject but the public at large which is something that should be avoided as much as possible. Operatives should remember that any distinctive behaviour will increase the chance of a memory trigger.

Figure 56 - Prime positioning on opposite side of the street

The other option is depicted in figure 56 where they are placed on the opposite side of the road of the entrance but not directly across from it. As mentioned earlier, the subject's arcs will more than likely be facing directly forward at least for a brief period of time whilst they exit the building, making it a poor position to be in. Instead they will be roughly opposite the prime positions that are across the road (mentioned above). One key thing to consider here are large vehicles that may block the line of sight thus increasing the risk of a loss.

Figure 57 - The downside of opposing prime positioning

SUMMARY

Prime positions are adopted dynamically as they are the least likely areas that the subject's paths are likely to cross thus, again reducing the likelihood of a compromise. There a several options that are available but the key impacting factors are as follows:

- The sit-rep
- The primary objectives
- Awareness level of the subject
- Previous observations
- Incidents during the current surveillance period
- Layout of the ground
- Level/ amount of foot traffic
- Level/ amount of road traffic
- Anticipated next direction of the subject.

TRIGGER SYSTEMS

This is a technique that is extremely beneficial for teams of any number exceeding one operative. It is useful for operations involving subjects who are more aware but can be implemented for any type as it enables the team to mount observations with only one operative being physically visible. In other words, apart from one operative, an entire team can be positioned where the subject is completely unable to see them. This works by having one operative in a location where they are able to observe the subject's expected departure location. This is always going to be building and is typically a known home address or work address but can in fact be set up for any building that the subject has entered if the team members are more experienced. The position is known as the 'trigger'. The name derives from how the role is performed. When the operative in this position observes the subject, they inform the rest of the team who are on standby. They 'trigger' the operation.

On the next page is an example for Op Luma where the client has provided intelligence that the subject is expected to leave a work related meeting in London (which is away from home) at 1730hrs where it is believed that he will meet an unknown female.

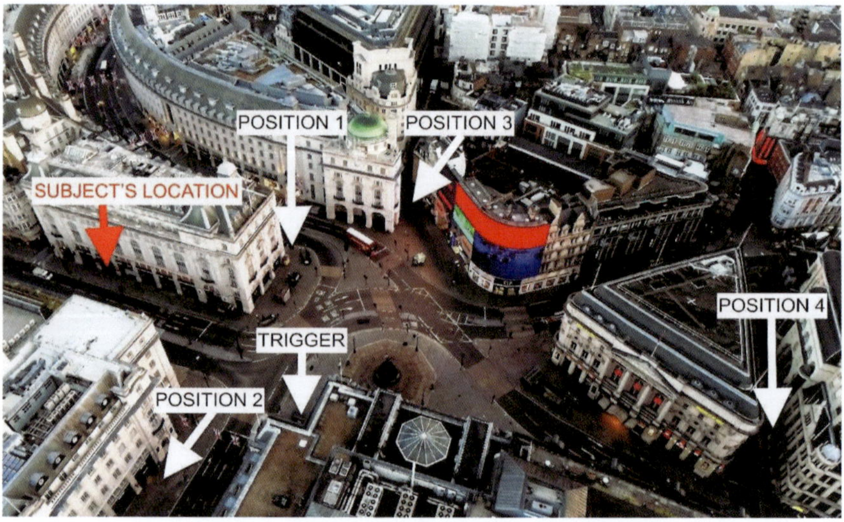

Figure 58 - Trigger system using foot surveillance operatives

The trigger operative does not necessarily need to be overt. They can be in a position that offers hard or soft cover to maintain a level of covert sustainability. If the layout of the ground permits, they can be positioned in a building mounting observations through an upper level window looking down. Only a hostile subject would possibly notice this. It is common practice for the trigger to be in a vehicle or a specially designated surveillance van.

Upon triggering the op, several pieces of information should be communicated to the other operatives. This includes;

- That the subject has departed
- MOT:
    - Are they on foot, in a vehicle, a taxi?

- In which direction they are heading:
    - If the team have been properly briefed and are fully prepared, the trigger will know the compass direction and the other operatives will know and be aware that the subject is heading in their direction. For example, "the subject has turned left heading east".
- Their attire:
    - A full but quick description of what the subject is wearing. Because of the urgency this will probably only include the main elements such as trousers, coat etc.
- Any other useful information:
    - This could include who they are with, are they carrying anything etc.

This message can be communicated in a number of ways but will more often than not be done verbally using a chat application or two way radios. Whilst it is relatively uncommon to use two way radios during a surveillance operation, if the team are in vehicles, it is easier to conceal the radios and therefore more acceptable.

Figure 59 Depicts an example of a trigger system being implemented for Op India Charlie where the team are mounting covert observations in an attempt to acquire evidence that the subject is not injured as they have stated in their insurance claim. This example demonstrates using both a mobile unit as well as foot operatives.

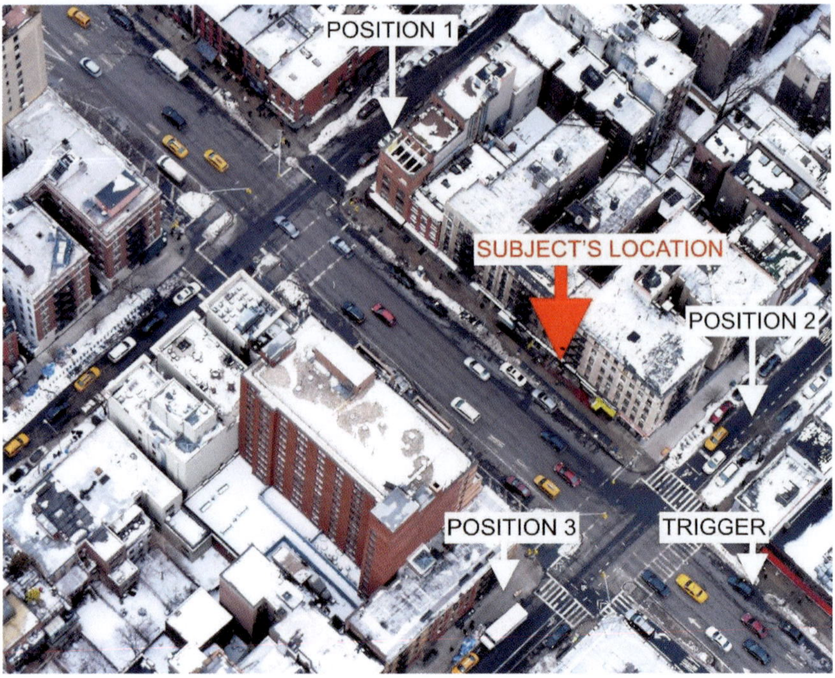

Figure 59 - A trigger system using a mobile unit and foot operatives

Below is an example of a verbal message that could be transmitted based on the scenario in figure 59. The operatives should have conducted regular 'comms checks' to ensure that they are in good working order.

TRIGGER - *"Subject has departed the HA and has turned right heading west on foot. He is wearing light blue jeans, and a red coat carrying a plastic bag."*

This message is brief but a good and realistic example of what is often sent to the team from the trigger position.

Without wishing to over complicate the trigger method, it is worth pointing out that it is possible to implement a system whereby the other team members can see the trigger but remain out of sight of the subject thus allowing the operation tobe triggered without using comms.

SUMMARY

A trigger can be on foot or in a vehicle. The deciding factor will be based on a number of variables including, the awareness of the subject, previous observations, the layout of the ground, number of operatives and more. Typically speaking (but not always), the trigger will be on foot if the subject is expected to travel by car. Conversely, if the subject is expected to travel by foot, the trigger will be based in a vehicle with the other team members on foot and out of sight. This is mainly because of the fact that the likelihood of the subject observing the trigger is somewhat mitigated based on the circumstances.

It is important to remember a trigger system can be implemented dynamically in the sense that, when a subject enters a building (even after the initial trigger), another one can be put in place to mitigate the risk of other operatives' falling within the subject's arcs thus being less likely to be compromised.

THE TIME/ DISTANCE METHOD

This method is designed to assist operatives locate a subject after losing visual contact for a short period of time. It works using three key ingredients, time, distance and the missing factor, speed. The measurement of distance is the hopeful outcome when using the other two elements in an attempt to locate the subject's whereabouts. For this to have a chance of working, the pace (speed) of the subject must first be assessed. This is arguably an implausible measurement and can be difficult to quantify therefore an average can be used instead. The operative must not lose control and exercise the so-called 'drip feed' so that their adrenaline does not get the better of them as the inevitable dump occurs. In order for this method to have any chance of working, the operative should have a relatively accurate idea of where they last observed the subject along with the time that has passed since that sighting, which should only be a matter of seconds at best a few minutes at worse. With these two elements combined (speed and time), the distance can be roughly measured. Whilst it is much easier to implement theoretically as opposed to practically, the method relies upon a large degree of level headedness.

Implementation

Once the subject has left the operative's field of vision, the operative must calculate the maximum distance that they could have travelled from that point (the distance). The only factor that is unknown, is the direction. Therefore, an area of uncertainty comes about which encompasses where the subject may be. This field is only relevant for the time in which the calculation was made. In other words, the subject could continue to advance in a certain direction and therefore, move out of that area.

On average, a human will walk between 2-3 meters per second. So, the operative must consider how far they could have travelled in the time from last sighting. Working on the assumption that it was ten seconds, the subject could be a maximum of thirty meters from the point of last observation. If this occurred in an open field, there would be no problem ascertaining the subject's location but in reality, they will quite possibly be in a number of buildings including shops, offices etc. Therefore, a process of elimination should be undertaken in an attempt to rule out any unlikely locations. Doing this should leave a smaller number of likely spots which then need to be explored. If part of a team, the chances of regaining sight of a subject are of course, considerably higher. A singular operative will have a harder time but remember that methods such as this are not a definitive practice, they are there to mitigate the likelihood of a loss.

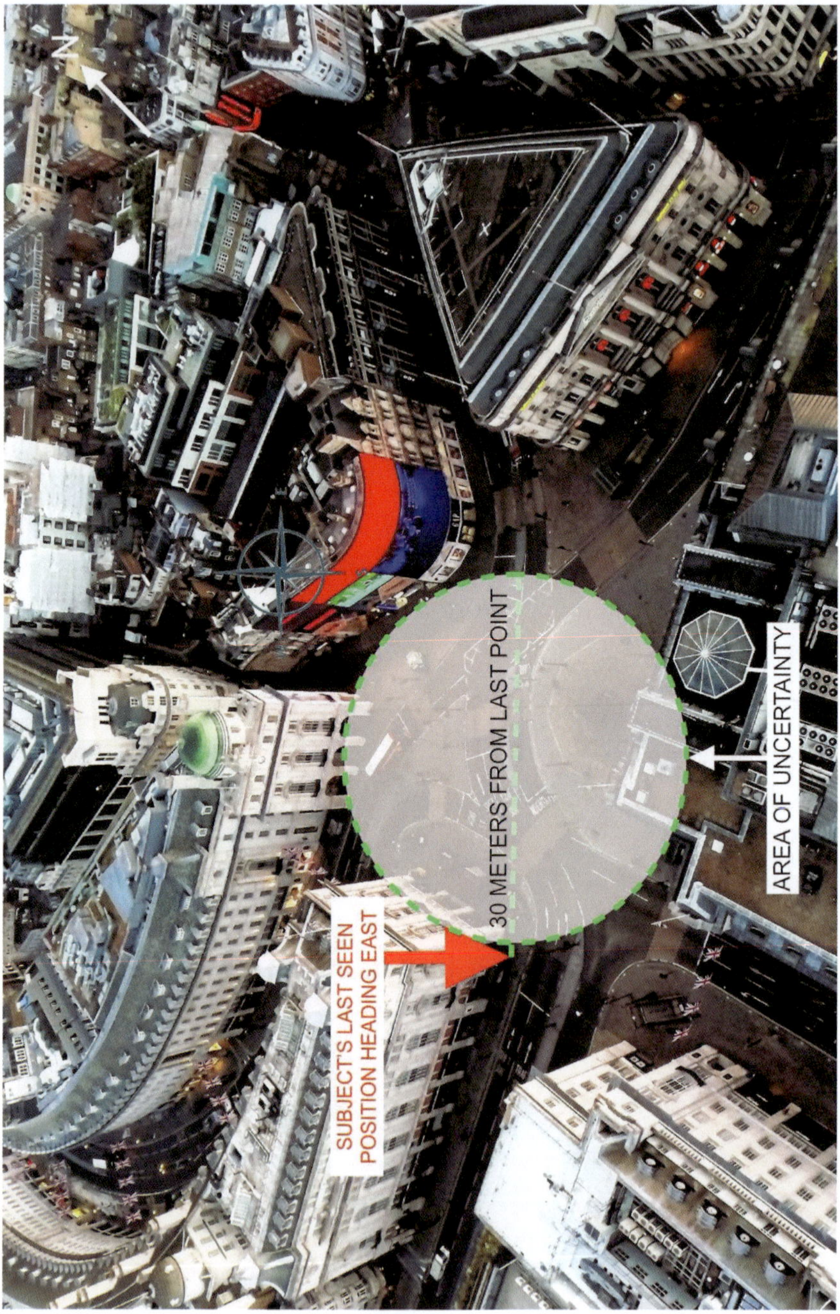

Figure 60 - The time/ distance method

OBSERVATION POINTS

Observation Points or (OPs) are a key reference point for those who operate in this field. Not to be confused with the abbreviation for 'operation(s), OPs are simply the locations in which operatives mount surveillance. This commonly used term is an alternative for 'positions' however, it is more frequently used for fixed locations often during operations that involve the use of mobile units (cars or surveillance vans) or when an operative remains static, usually in a building. For this reason, triggers can be said to be in an OP.

The term is more commonly used in sub-urban or remote environments when camoflauge is employed where the position is known as a 'green OP'.

Figure 61 - Green OP (Adamgrimm.com, 2020)

Owing to the fact that previous chapters have discussed external positions, this one will briefly consider how OPs can be implemented on specific types of tasks. A new fictitious operation will be introduced in order to demonstrate how an observation point may be useful.

Due to a threat issued to their principal, a security firm client has instructed the investigation company to identify who is responsible. A vehicle has been observed following the principal (along with being seen parked close to the HA and WA) and a VRN has been recorded. The investigation company then implement Operation Charlie Sierra, a counter surveillance op to establish where the vehicle regularly visits. The vehicle appears to be housed at a private residence overnight for a majority of the week. The security company's instructions were to identify who is responsible, not where the vehicle is parked overnight or even where it is registered. At this stage names are not required, only images so that they can be distributed between the security team so that they can identify them as a potential threat if observed whilst the client is out on the ground. Because of this, intelligence relating to the occupants is required in order to better protect the principal. This does not require any individual to be followed. Instead, only a record/ report (including imagery) of all individuals who enter and exit the building. Therefore, a singular observation point is required. This can be facilitated by the use of an opposing building or a surveillance van. If the building has multiple entrances/ exits, several OPs can be implemented.

Figure 62 - A building with multiple entrances and exits

MOBILE SURVEILLANCE

Mobile

adjective

adjective: mobile

1.able to move or be moved freely or easily.

Unit

or 'units' typically refer to vehicles whether that be motorcycles, cars or vans to assist the facilitation of a covert surveillance operation.

As with most surveillance related topics, the use of mobile units on a covert operation is subjective to a number of factors. These include:

- The sit-rep
- The primary objectives
- Awareness level of the subject
- Previous observations
- Incidents during the current surveillance period
- Layout of the ground
- Level/ amount of foot traffic
- Level/ amount of road traffic
- Anticipated movements of the subject

The most important factor which is not included in that list is the MOT (method of transportation). Consider an operative attempting to mount observations on a subject who typically travels to work on a motorbike. An investigation organisation, whether that be private or otherwise, should endeavour to acquire such intelligence to establish how the subject may travel prior to the surveillance period commencing. If that information is unattainable, there are several options to overcome this;

1. **Reconnaissance** - A thorough recce op may indicate what transportation options are available to the subject.
2. **Research** - Speaking to the client, intelligence source or utilising other means of identifying how the subject may travel from A to B.
3. **Prepare for all possible outcomes** - If the budget allows, having mobile units as well as foot operatives will almost always be beneficial.

With respect to the last option, the type of 'mobile unit' is up for some level of debate. There is no definitive science as to which is best. This is mainly owing to the multitude of elements that may have an affect on the operation however, it could be argued that an operative on a motorbike is far more favourable in most situations because of the maneuverability that it offers.

Static or Mobile?

One of the many advantages of utilising mobile units as a wider part of a covert surveillance operation is that they can be both static or mobile. Why would a mobile unit remain static? One answer is, to accommodate a trigger. I have personally worked on many tasks as the trigger (especially earlier on in my career when I was the youngest on the task). The reason for this is, the entire operation depends on this position and so the pressure at the beginning is huge. When there is no indication as to when the subject is due to depart their given location, an operative acting as the trigger could be responsible for staring at the same doorway for hours on end without the opportunity to eat, drink or a toilet break. Remember, an entire team is relying on that individual's ability to observe, communicate and relay key information that will allow the task to properly commence.

Once the trigger has performed their rather brief role of announcing the departure of a subject, they quite often become redundant as a result of being concealed in a surveillance van, potentially for prolonged periods of time. The operative cannot leave the van without compromising their position. This can be hot, tiring, and extremely uncomfortable if not properly prepared which perhaps explains why the youngest member is often bullied into (I mean encouraged) into taking up this position.

Provisions for Surveillance Vans

As a result of performing this role, I am able to offer a few tips or considerations;

1. **Food and water** - it is extremely important to have enough food and water to last the duration of the task.
2. **Means of communicating** - As the trigger, it is vital that the operative in this position has either a two way radio signal to use a mobile chat application or any other form of comms to send out the relevant information. This is also important in case of an emergency.
3. **The call of nature** - Not wishing to sound vulgare, a bottle with a wide opening for number ones and some cling film for number twos should be made available.

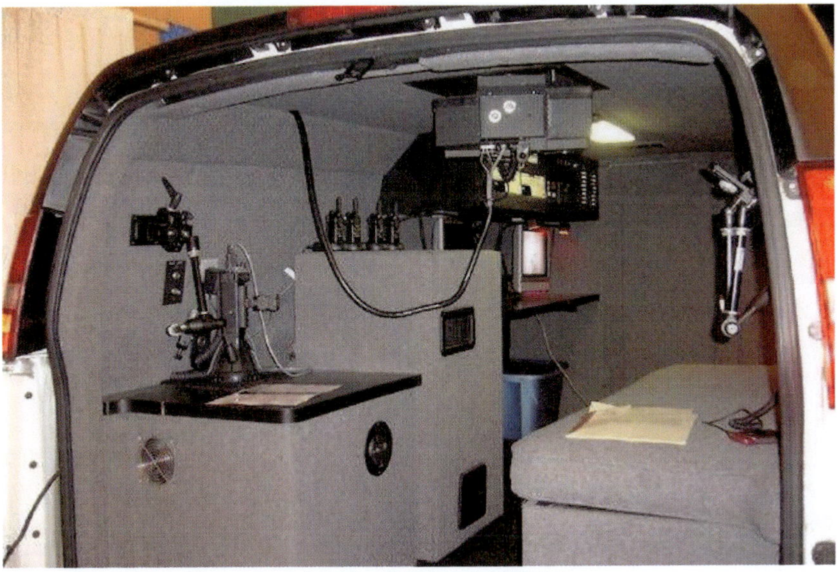

Figure 63 - Surveillance van interior (Pintrest, 2020b)

Modifications

Any van can, in theory, be converted into one that is designated for the purposes of surveillance:

Generic in Design - Much like operatives, surveillance vans should be generic in their appearance avoiding anything that may give someone cause to remember it.

Concealment - Given that some vans have windows, it is wise to ensure that all measures have been taken to prevent anyone from being able to see inside the vehicle.

Bulkhead separation - Many commercial vehicles have this by default. It is a large piece of material (often wood) that is situated just behind the seats in the front cabin and the rear compartment of the van. This is relevant because it is important to have some form of cut out window that acts as a viewing point or window. However, rather than just having a square hole in the bulkhead, there will be one way glass or plastic so as to maintain the appearance of a standard van.

Camera mount(s) - It is very common for a van to have camera mounts fixed close to observation ports. These can be utilised for both SLR or video cameras given that all cameras have the same universal screw hole designed for camera mounts and tripods.

Additional batteries - A standard vehicle battery does not last very long when the engine is not running, especially when it is being used to power items such as laptops, phones etc.

Power source(s) - Cameras, phones, laptops, comms and any other devices will require charging. Having additional power sources or at the very least, power banks, are an absolute must to ensure a successful operation.

Window wiper switch - Should the weather take a turn for the worse, the operative's vision may be impaired. Being in the back of the vehicle away from the switches, it is practically impossible for him or her to reach the switches in the front. It is, therefore, a good idea to have one that is accessible in the rear. Many contest that this could potentially compromise the van as an unoccupied vehicle with the window wipers activating is an unnatural occurrence. On the other hand, how long does the window wipers take to make one stroke?

Blower fan switch - If it does rain outside or become too hot inside, it is viable that the windows will become steamed which again, will compromise the operative's view. A fan switch will overcome this issue fairly easily.

Comfort - Given that an operative may be sat in the rear of a van for a prolonged period of time, cushions, sleeping bags, air conditioner, fan, heater and a chair are all nice things to have available. The chair (or seat) should be adjustable so as to suit the required height to allow the operative to aim the camera in the right direction without undue discomfort.

Coil spring clamps - In an effort to restrict the van from moving whilst its occupants manoeuvre around inside, spring clamps can be applied. In essence, they immobilise the suspension system and thus the movement of the van which could of course compromise its position. It is not advisable to drive too far with the clamps applied as it is extremely uncomfortable and could damage any equipment within.

Health and Safety - Being in a relatively confined space made of pressed steel and surrounded by auxiliary electrical facilities can pose a risk. For this reason basic precautions should be taken. A valid fire extinguisher that can be used to tackle electrical fires is vital. The most common form at the time of writing this book comes in the form of a powder extinguisher. The owner of the van should also ensure that there is a safe exit route; a way for the operative to get out of the vehicle if required.

Implementation

A surveillance van is relatively straightforward to put into position. This is usually achieved by having one operative park the vehicle in the desired location whilst the operative remains in the back. There should be some dialogue to ensure that there is a clear line of vision from the operative in the rear to wherever (or whatever) they are responsible for monitoring.

Cars

The use of cars is extremely common in covert surveillance operations owing to the simple fact that most people have one and for most tasks, are usable. There are a number of relatively minor alterations that can be made to a vehicle in order to make it more serviceable for this line of work:

Concealed dash cams - Trying to hold a phone or camera to record video footage whilst driving is dangerous. Many years ago, certain operatives would have a professional camera mount screwed into their dashboard which, as many would agree, is not very subtle. With the size of cameras available to us in this day and age, there is no reason why a covert camera cannot be installed in some way into the vehicle's dashboard or 'A pillar'. The 'A pillar' is the structural connection between the roof and the bonnet (or hood).

Bumper cams - Cameras can be concealed into other parts of the vehicle including the bumpers so as to provide a range of angles. The imagery/ footage can be utilised for evidence/ report writing purposes.

Inverter - An inverter will allow the user to convert (or invert) power from a 12v power source which is found in most vehicles, to that required for domestic purposes. This includes chargers for laptops, camera equipment, two way radios or any other such devices.

Tinted windows - Tinted or blacked out windows will offer a far more concealable vehicle however, there are some things that need to be considered here; firstly, does it attract unnecessary attention? Secondly, are there any legal restrictions on having blacked out windows? Conversely, in the UK it is illegal for the front windows on a private vehicle to let any less than 70% of light through.

Positioning

The positions adopted by mobile units will of course depend on a wide range of factors. These have been mentioned in previous chapters and include but are not limited to:

- The sit-rep
- The primary objectives
- The awareness level of the subject
- Previous observations
- Incidents during the current surveillance period
- Layout of the ground
- Level/ amount of foot traffic (both inside and outside of the building)
- Level/ amount of road traffic (outside of the building)
- Anticipated next direction/ movements of the subject.

Figure 64 depicts how a mobile unit may be used as a trigger in conjunction with operatives on foot. This combination would only be used when the subject is expected to travel on foot.

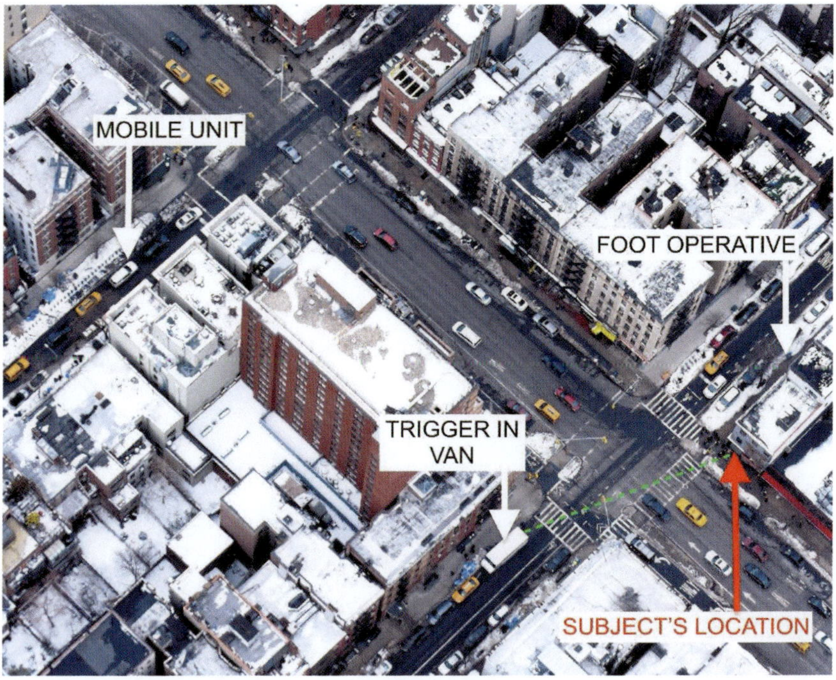

Figure 64 - A trigger system using mobile units

Figure 65 - Prime positioning being utilised for mobile surveillance

Generally speaking, the vehicle (car or van) should be located in a way that replicates that of a prime position relative to where the subject is expected to depart from. This will reduce the likelihood of the vehicle standing out or being noticed or standing out. (See figure 65)

If there is availability to park anywhere, a few factors should be taken into consideration when deciding where to mount observations from.

Direction of the sun - Where possible, the vehicle should be parked with the sun behind it. This will mitigate the risk of the operative inside being observed as the subject's pupils will contract making it far more difficult to notice minor details. Also, if the sun is facing the operative, they will be highlighted with reduced vision for the same reason as above.

Figure 66 - The difficulty when looking toward the sun (Tantek.com, 2020)

Camera angles - The operative should ensure that they have the ability to take covert imagery.

Internal reflections - This is a reflection on the inside of the windows of the vehicle that will have a negative impact on photography. This could be something on the dashboard that reflects on the inside of the windscreen affecting autofocus and the colouring of a photograph.

External reflections - This is anything that reflects light from within the vehicle, out. For example, a reflective pair of sunglasses (mirrored lenses) or a shiny bracelet. There is nothing more noticeable to the human eye than a flashing light, so it is wise to ensure external reflections are avoided. It is not uncommon for operatives to put electrical tape around their cameras because they have metallic or shiny surfaces on them.

Camera flash - An easy thing to overlook but for obvious reasons, it is extremely important to ensure that the flash is switched 'off' and not to 'auto'.

State of the vehicle - The vehicle should be in keeping with its surroundings. This will further mitigate the chances of it standing out. Generally speaking most vehicles will suit most areas however, it is worth considering those scenarios where a brand new Mercedes would stand out or that on the other end of the scale.

Third parties - It is advisable to avoid, where possible, parking outside of the home of someone whose attention may be attracted by the mere fact that an unfamiliar van or a vehicle with someone sat in it for a prolonged period of time, is outside their living room window.

Other Considerations

Clothing - As discussed in the 'Human brain and peripheral awareness' chapter, the operative should wear dark, nondescript clothing. In this instance, it will allow them to blend in with the vehicle's interior more than if they were to wear something lighter in colour.

Controlling adrenaline - Utilising the method of Cooper's colour codes is a good idea. I can say from personal experience that operatives will and do experience a dump of adrenaline when they observe the subject for the first time. In addition to that, if they are surprised by the action of someone who they are not focusing on, a series of unplanned actions are likely to follow leading to a loss of focus. Considering each step of a set of pre-planned actions on drills will allow the operative to overcome this.

A safe exit route - Ensuring that there is a safe route to drive away from is absolutely vital. It is imperative that the operative is able to safely drive away should a hostile incident occur. This means facing the right way in dead end streets, knowing the way out of a complex street layout along with any other safety consideration.

SUMMARY

The success of many operations will depend upon photography or video footage of the subject entering and/ or leaving a specific building. Following a subject in a vehicle is a difficult undertaking to achieve. If the roads are quiet then it is difficult not to be seen and if the roads are busy, it is practically impossible to keep up with the subject owing to traffic, traffic lights, human traffic and many other factors. If there are two or more vehicles following a subject vehicle, the chances of a loss can be reduced slightly but this will require constant communication and a good level of training.

The chances are, one vehicle will be following a subject's vehicle at any one time. Therefore, the tactics adopted are somewhat restricted. The use of vehicle tracking devices is really the only way to ensure that the team do not suffer a loss during the observation period. This convenient option will require some research to ensure that the use of such is legal. The safest way to physically follow a mobile vehicle whilst using a tracking device is to have two operatives in one vehicle; one driving and the other monitoring the live location and providing the driver with directions.

Motorcycles are, in most settings, the ideal tool to facilitate mobile surveillance. Not only are most nondescript, they are far more agile than cars or vans. A trained and licenced (where required) surveillance operative with a motorbike is a valuable asset.

SURVEILLANCE LOGS

Over the following paragraphs, we will briefly consider the use of what are commonly referred to as surveillance logs, their influence on final reports and how they can be replaced. Surveillance logs are in essence, a way of briefly denoting the movements of a subject or activity relating to a specific location. The chronological list allows the operative(s) to write down all eventualities combined with timings in a way that can be referred to later on. Historically, this is done on pen and paper, and in many cases, probably still is. With a narrow column on the left hand side and the rest reserved for notes (or logs), this is a document that can be revised when compiling the final surveillance report.

Please see below an example of how a surveillance log may appear for Op Luma

Start Time: 1737hrs

Operation: Op Luma

Address/ Location: 5 Roger Street, Manchester M1 4EN

1737hrs	Black Ford Focus (SE16 URE) leaves property. One unknown male driver (IC1) - no other occupants.
1736hrs	IC1 Male driver returns to property on foot.
1804hrs	Unknown female enters the property on foot.
1902hrs	Subject exits property on foot - turns left. Unaccompanied.
1942hrs	No further movements observed.

This log will later be put into a final surveillance report so that you can observe the difference more clearly.

In the public sector, police officers or other public servants may use their pocket notebooks to compile a surveillance log.

Here is another example for Op India Charlie

Start Time: 1300hrs

Operation: Op India Charlie

Address/ Location: 31 West 34th Street, New York, NY 10001

1332hrs	Subject departs HA turning right heading west on foot. (image taken)
1404hrs	Subject enters ABC gym
1501hrs	Subject leaves gym
1512hrs	Subject enters fitness supplement store.
1520hrs	Subject exits fitness supplement store carrying two large bags.
1543hrs	Subject enters HA

Because logs denote the time, any imagery taken from the operation can be later reconciled so that there is accompanying imagery for each entry. This is made a lot easier if the settings on the camera are set so that the correct time is either stamped on the images or is viewable on the camera when reviewing them. It may also be a good idea for the operative to synchronise the time on their camera with that on their watch to ensure accurate reporting.

SUMMARY

Logs are a brief summary of the subject's movements. It will be primarily utilised by the operative as a reference when compiling their final report. In some situations the log itself may be used as evidence and should therefore always be factually accurate.

REPORT WRITING

Reports are a very important aspect of any service within the security and investigation industry. In many cases, they are the only tangible material that the client will receive after paying for a service. Surveillance is a good example of this. If a surveillance operation is instructed by a client, they will receive a full report accompanied by images. It is always good practice to assume that all reports are going to be used as evidence in court. This way, it will become second nature to write them in the correct manner.

Before outlining all of what *should* be included in a report, let us first consider a number of things that should be excluded.

Firstly, reports have to be a statement of fact, not assumption. For example, we absolutely cannot say something like “I think he entered a grey vehicle”. This would invite the subject’s defense (if in court) to question the integrity of the operative and consequently damage the credibility of the report they have written. The statement should read something to the effect of, “I observed the subject entering a vehicle, I believe the vehicle was grey in colour”. We must be 100% accurate in what we say to be truthful. Another example would be “the subject entered a grey Volkswagen”. If it transpires that it was not a VW, then again the whole integrity of that report will be held in question and deemed as useless. This may anger the client and make the operative appear incompetent.

Secondly, the general public do not use the jargon or terminology mentioned at the beginning of this book and should therefore be disregarded from any report apart from a few, minor exceptions. To put this into context, imagine that you are unfamiliar with any surveillance or military based jargon, and then reading a report describing a subject's movements as, "CHANDLER then left the HA turning left onto Main Street ......". It would make no sense. The few minor exceptions will become apparent when you read the example reports provided over the coming pages.

In addition to the paragraphs above, the report should not appear as a carbon copy or neater version of a surveillance log. Instead it needs to be more detailed, user friendly and understandable whilst avoiding exaggeration or false/ bold statements. Remember, that this is the private sector and clients expect to receive as much detail as possible.

Another common mistake is the disclosure of the operative's position. In other words denoting, within the content of the report, where he/ she were mounting their observations from. From my experience this can lead to the client questioning why this observation point was adopted as opposed to one that they themselves may have chosen, despite the fact that they are not trained by any means, in this field. To save the requirement for lengthy explanations, operatives are encouraged to leave this information out of their reports. There are no legal requirements for it to be referenced in a report. That is not to say that an operative should not be conscious of their positioning, quite the opposite. If a case was to go as far as court and a surveillance report was to be used as evidence, then the defence may want to question where the operative was located at the time the report refers to, in an effort to discredit a specific entry/ statement or the report in its entirety.

Before outlining the basic composition of a report, I would first like to take you back through a history of my report writing training. This is relevant because it highlights particulars from both the public and private sector. I was fortunate enough to have what might be considered a relatively unique experience in that I was writing reports/ statements in the RMP and the private sector almost simultaneously. That is, one week I was away with the army writing statements relating to RTCs (road traffic collisions) and the following week, writing surveillance reports for operations taking place across the globe.

Something that struck me as interesting, pretty much straight away was the stringent control in which the police took on the pocket notebooks that are formally issued to officers of both military and civilian police forces across the land. Not only are they serialised, they are considered an official document. The mere fact that they are referred to as a 'document' should affirm their level of solemnity, let alone 'officiality'. Officers are required to record information that may be required as evidence. Any entry must be followed by a line that prevents any additional information being put in later on.

At one point in my career, I worked as 'Head of International

Surveillance Ops'. I was tasked with overseeing surveillance tasks in whichever country they were taking place on behalf of the company that I was working for. I engaged contractors as freelance surveillance operatives, passing on live intelligence to clients and senior figures within the organisation and proofreading reports. On many occasions during this time, I was given basic surveillance logs and images from operations across the UK and sometimes overseas, from non-English speaking contractors. It was my job to interpret them and compile a report that was verifiable with the evidence. In other words, I composed reports using the times stated in the logs along with general information or recorded movements that matched those timings. These two items of information combined (timings and information) made up what we refer to as an 'entry'. I then had to include the imagery to back up what the entry stated. Once compiled, the report was sent to the operative to ensure that it corroborated with what they had observed before being forwarded to the client.

Reports must be taken seriously when composing them. As mentioned previously, a report is a statement and can be later used as evidence. Anything mentioned within a report must be accurate and, when possible, backed up with evidence.

The Basic Information Required for any Report

Date

The format for the date can vary depending on your own

personal preferred choice but my preference is 26/06/2013 or 06/26/2013 if you are in the US.

Timings

The format that we use is the 24 hour clock with hrs (short for hours) next to it. For example,
2pm would appear as 1400hrs. Conversely, “hrs’ is one of the only terms that we use in a briefing that can also be used in a report.

Locations

The full address including postcodes or zip codes of where the operation started along with any addresses that the subject visited during the surveillance period.

During the training programmes, the candidates are tasked with covertly following a subject for a relatively prolonged period of time over quite a distance through the busy foot and road traffic of the busy city centres where the courses take place. This is a difficult undertaking owing to the many factors that affect such a task, not to mention the fact that it is, more often than not, their first time mounting covert observations. At the end of their first task, they are asked to create a log of all addresses visited which is to be inclusive of timings. The more experienced candidates may only find this slightly difficult but for a majority, it is almost impossible.

Fortunately, there are several ways in which this can be made easier. One option is to download a running/ jogging app of which one of its functions is to track where the device has travelled. This does not highlight which buildings the subject may have entered but it will denote where the end user of the app slowed down or stopped. The other downside to this is that it will drain the battery on the phone.

Another method, and the one that I recommend, is to take covert imagery of each building that he/ she enters and when possible, a street sign. As detailed later on in this section, imagery is extremely important. In addition to its importance for reporting purposes, it enables the operative to review the imagery and acquire the full address of each location once combined with some brief online research. Alternatively, the location settings can be adjusted to allow images to have location information accessible when reviewing the imagery or footage.

Imagery or Diagrams

Surveillance reports are typically comprised of images. There are, however, going to be times when you are unable to acquire the imagery required to accompany your entry. As an alternative, you can use a diagram that will either denote the layout of the ground and the subject's movements or a screenshot of a map from which you can do the same. It is, of course, preferable to use imagery that you have taken. Operatives who form part of a team of two or more team members, should only use imagery they have taken themselves. This is to prevent images being used in different reports.

Entry
An entry denoting something that happened in the time mentioned. An entry is the section that contains a description. For a surveillance report, it is not uncommon for the first entry to be constructed using a 'template entry' or 'template statement'. This is because most surveillance operations will begin at either a home address (HA) or work address (WA) and can therefore be inclusive of generic details such as the address, why the operative is at this address, a description of the building, any vehicles that may be associated either to the property or the subject.

During my training programmes, we discuss the following example template:

*At **1) TIME**hrs, I arrive at **2) FULL ADDRESS, 3) WHY THIS ADDRESS? (4) Subject first Name LAST NAME**), where my observations commence. **4) DESCRIPTION OF BUILDING/ LOCATION.***

5) ANY ADDITIONAL INFORMATION PERTAINING TO THE LOCATION?

Example first entry using template above:
At 1206hrs, I arrive at 27 Austin Friars, London EC2N 2QP, the known work address of the subject (Michael CHANDLER), where my observations commence. I would describe the building as a large Victorian terrace, purpose built office at least

three stories high.

Upon arrival, I observed a grey Mercedes E-Class (VRN: SE16 URE) parked directly outside the building.

The Subject

Observe how the subject is referred to in this example. It is good practice for the first name to be written normally with their surname or family name being written in capitals. This is something that is transferred from the public to the private sector.

In some of the example reports that are to follow, you will notice that some operatives continue to refer to the subject, simply as 'the subject' whilst others will use the subject's family name. At any point during a report that the subject's surname is used, it should always be written in capitals. This comes down to preference. However, it is best practice to mention their full name in the first entry so that it is clear whom the subject is from the outset.

Hollywood movies tend to refer to a subject as a 'target' and so do many operatives. I would advise against this for a number of reasons. Namely that, a target is something that you aim a weapon at. The person whom an operative is mounting covert observations upon is not someone whom they intend to aim weapons at or, indeed cause any harm. Instead they are the subject of enquiry upon whom they are monitoring for intelligence acquisition purposes.

Start Time: 1737hrs Operation: Op Luma

1737hrs	I arrive at 5 Roger Street, Manchester M1 4EN, the known work address of the subject, where my observations commence. I would describe the building as a converted set of portacabins, grey in colour, which form part of a small industrial compound. There are several other businesses operating within the compound including a skip company, car repair garage and a furniture removals service. The compound is square in shape and has both a vehicle entrance gate and a foot entrance gate both of which are locked during out of business hours.
1736hrs	I observe a Black Ford Focus (VRN: SE16 URE) leave the property turning right heading north. There was one occupant, an unknown male driver. I would describe the driver as a white male aged between 30-40 years of age with dark coloured short hair.
1804hrs	I observe the unknown male driver return to property on foot. The male appeared to walk in the direction from which he drove the vehicle. At this point the male was wearing what I would describe as white trainers, dark coloured jeans and a black and red checkered shirt. I would estimate the male to be approximately 6 feet tall.
1902hrs	An unknown female enters the property on foot approaching it from a northerly direction. I would describe the female as a slim white, aged between 35-40 years old with long blonde hair and wearing what I would describe as brown ankle boots, black skinny jeans and a denim shirt.
1942hrs	I observe the subject (Daniel SMITH) exit the property on foot turning left on Roger Street heading North. SMITH was unaccompanied and can be described as approximately 6 feet tall, well built wearing what I would describe as brown Chelsea boots, light denim jeans and a white shirt with a navy blue suit jacket.
2000hrs	I observe no further movements at this time. Observations terminated.

Start Time: 1300hrs Operation: Op India Charlie

1300hrs	I arrive at 31 West 34th Street, New York, NY 10001, the known home address of the subject, where my observations commence. I would describe the building as a large town building with a stone facade. The glass door entrance is between two retail units with what I would describe as light coloured cladding.
1332hrs	I observe the subject depart the building via the front door of the property turing right heading in a westerly direction on foot. I would describe the subject as a white male, with light brown hair, short to medium length. I would estimate him to be approximately 5' 10" (imperial) and of an athletic build with no visible distinctive marks. The subject was wearing what I would describe as running shoes/ trainers, navy blue shorts with a white Nike tick on the lower left leg and a plain white t-shirt. He was also carrying what I would describe as a black back pack over his left shoulder.
1404hrs	Subject enters ABC Gym via the main entrance.
1501hrs	Subject departs the same gym via the main entrance and appears to have exercised due to what appears to be a significant amount of sweat on the white t-shirt. The subject then walks the most direct route to GNC fitness supplement store located at 600 8th Ave, New York, NY 10018.
1512hrs	The subject enters the fitness supplement store.
1520hrs	Subject exits GNC fitness supplement store carrying two large bags in addition to the back pack. Upon leaving, the subject walks a direct route to the known home address.
1543hrs	Subject enters the home address with the two large carrier bags and backpack.

SUMMARY

This book covers a range of techniques that can be utilised both on foot and when mobile. The list is by no means extensive and there is no doubt that you will learn others along your journey as a surveillance operative. Covert surveillance is often a long and boring endeavour with hours spent watching a front door with no movement whatsoever. However, once the subject is observed or something similar occurs, there is no feeling like it. There will be a dump of adrenaline which requires a conscious degree of control and this book has discussed how that can be achieved.

Many of these methods can be used in conjunction with one another in a wide range of combinations. For example, a team can trigger a surveillance operation when a subject leaves their home address. When that subject enters a shop, the team can then implement another trigger system with the trigger operative utilising prime positioning. This takes an extensive amount of teamwork and communication, all of which is developed over time.

Being a surveillance operative does not automatically give the individual a right to the title Private Investigator. A PI is a completely different role that utilises covert surveillance as part of its intelligence acquisition or fact verification process. A covert operative is arguably the first step in the investigative career route.

Whilst being a surveillance operative can instigate a career of its own, it is a vital skill set for anyone who is professionally responsible for the security of another individual. The first page of the book states the following:

Understanding the intricacies of foot and mobile surveillance is a vital attribute for any close protection officer. Knowing how covert operatives / teams function, methods of communication, the foot drills that they adopt, is key and can only really be understood by someone who has been trained to a high standard. Without it, your principal will be vulnerable to surveillance whether that be hostile reconnaissance or covert intelligence acquisition relating to their daily movements (pattern of life) in an effort to establish weak points within the security arrangements. Identifying such activities will mitigate this risk considerably thus providing a far more secure environment for them.

As an occupation, surveillance cannot be taught by reading only. The harsh reality is that practical training is required. Despite this, there is an online course available utilising a series of videos demonstrating the various tactics. Anyone who decides to enrol on this virtual training programme will be invited to attend the full five day advanced surveillance course at a discounted rate. There they will partake in practical operations using actors in major city centres to make it as realistic as possible. My close protection course with Vanquish® incorporates surveillance and personal protection to demonstrate, in a realistic setting, how the two overlap.

I would like to take this opportunity to thank you for taking the time to read this book. Moreover, please accept my gratitude for buying it. You may or not be aware that all proceeds will go to my charity The Vanquish Foundation. This is also the case for my other publication *Technical Surveillance Countermeasures* apart from the Australian Edition for which the profits go to Sydney based charity Mates on a Mission.

Please see below the information about the charity from the website:

The foundation was set up to provide all that is required in order to facilitate the advancement of education of homeless veterans with a specified aim of assisting them to gain the qualifications and licence(s) that will allow them to seek employment. This will be achieved with the assistance of Vanquish® Training Academy who will grant free spaces on scheduled courses.

Vanquish® Training Academy run security related courses from which candidates gain accredited qualifications that enable them to apply for the necessary SIA licence that is required to work in the security industry.

For the public benefit, we will endeavour to raise funds to cover the cost of accommodation, clothing, learning materials and all other items that are required to enable someone to undergo this form of training. Once qualified and licensed, we will seek free, professional advice in relation to CV writing and other skills that will assist the beneficiaries gain employment. We will also liaise with employers in the security industry in an effort to have them agree to consider our beneficiaries.

On behalf of myself and The Vanquish Foundation, thank you.

Continuous Professional Development

CPD is a very important aspect of any professional career. It relates to the constant development of the knowledge and expertise of any given field. In the context of surveillance, it would be inclusive of legislation because any professional should know how the law impacts their work and be aware of what is considered lawful and unlawful and new equipment that is available that may make it easier for the operative to carry out their duties.

Online Course

This course has been converted into an online course which is inclusive of powerpoint presentations, visual demonstrations, downloadable content and assessments. In order to give you a feel for how the training programme is delivered online, we have created a free trial consisting of randomly selected video video lessons and a mock assessment

If this is something that is of interest to you, please go to www.TheSecurity.Academy for more information

Connecting with me

Despite the industry I work in, I have made a conscious decision to make my profile available and have open pages on Facebook, Instagram as well as a blog site which I implore you to follow.

Instagram - https://Instagram.com/michaelchandlersecurity
Facebook - https://Facebook.com/michaelchandlersec
Blog - https://MichaelChandler.Online

REFERENCES

LEGISLATION

Health and Safety at Work Act 1974 s 2 and s 7
Human Rights Act 1998 art 8
The Regulation of Investigatory Powers Act 2000
Protection from Harassment Act 1997
Regulation of Investigatory Powers Act 2000

WEBSITES

Relevant Legislation. Available at https://www.Legislation.gov.uk

Daily Mail Online 2012. Available at https://www.dailymail.co.uk/tvshowbiz/article-2121011/Matthew-Morrison-Chace-Crawford-enjoy-night-London.html

Lawmate 2020a - https://www.lawmate.com/style/Frame/m5/product.asp?customer_id=2846&lang=2&content_set=color_3&name_id=139415&page=2

Lawmate 2020b - https://www.amazon.com/Lawmate-Covert-Hidden-Glasses-PV-EG20CL/dp/B079F19NX8

Pinterest 2019a - Front wheel suspension assembly. Available at https://www.pinterest.co.uk/pin/509891989035661835/

Digital Photography School, 2020 - Available at https://digital-photography-school.com/megapost-learning-how-to-use-your-first-dslr/

JerichoDomingo 2020 - A shopping centre layout. Available at https://jerichodomingo.blogspot.com/2018/08/shopping-center-conceptual-3d-floor-plan.html

Adamgrimm.com, 2020 - A green OP. Available at https://www.adamgrimm.com/reference

Pinterest, 2020b - Surveillance van interior. Available at https://www.pinterest.co.uk/pin/190417890469385867/

antek.com, 2020 - The difficulty when looking toward the sun. Available at https://tantek.com/2020/062/t1/

https;//VanquishAcademy.com/close-protection-training

https://TheSecurity.Academy

https://MichaelChandler.Online

Printed in Great Britain
by Amazon

26812733R00123